Emotionally Healthy
Relationships

Day by Day

Emotionally Healthy Relationships
Day by Day

A 40-DAY JOURNEY *to* DEEPLY
CHANGE YOUR RELATIONSHIPS

Peter Scazzero

ZONDERVAN

Emotionally Healthy Relationships Day by Day
Copyright © 2017 by Peter Scazzero

Requests for information should be addressed to:
Zondervan, *3900 Sparks Dr. SE, Grand Rapids, Michigan 49546*

ISBN 978-0-310-34959-4 (softcover)

ISBN 978-0-310-34960-0 (ebook)

Author is represented by The Christopher Ferebee Agency, www.christopherferebee.com

Cover photo: Andrew Kuzmin / Shutterstock®
Interior design: Kait Lamphere

First Printing June 2017 / Printed in the United States of America

20 21 PC/LSCH 15

To June Eileen Sunquist

Contents

Acknowledgments

I want to begin by acknowledging the pioneering work of Benedict of Nursia, the sixth-century Italian monk, for making widely available to the Western Church the practice of the Daily Office. And I am grateful to the Trappist monks of St. Joseph's Abbey in Spencer, Massachusetts, who first offered me a lived experience of the beauty and power of stopping to be with God multiple times a day during a 2003 weeklong retreat.

I also want to acknowledge Christine Anderson for the rich combination of editorial gifts she brought to this project. Her eye for consistency and fractures in my logic made it a much better, and richer, devotional. Thank you, Christine, for consistently pushing me to be a better writer. Thanks also to Greg Clouse at Zondervan for carrying this *EH Relationships Day by Day* to completion, bringing a patient, careful, editorial eye to detail.

The Emotionally Healthy Spirituality team at Zondervan have been wonderful partners over the years. A special thanks to Sandy Vander Zicht, John Raymond, Tom Dean, Ryan Pazdur, Beth Murphy, and David Morris. Your love for Christ and publishing expertise is a gift to the work of God around the world.

And finally, a thank you to Geri, my lovely wife and best friend. Thank you, Geri, for being the most godly, amazing woman I know.

Loving Others Begins with Loving God

A number of years ago, a friend who had quit attending church asked me privately, "Why is it that so many Christians make such lousy human beings?" In other words, why are so many of us judgmental, defensive, and touchy?

I believe part of the reason stems from the fact that we so readily compartmentalize loving God from loving others. This was something the religious leaders in Jesus' day did as well. They were diligent and zealous to love God, but they were not equally diligent and zealous to love people. This put them on a collision course with Jesus. Toward the end of his ministry, Jesus summarized the entire Bible for them with these words: "'Love the Lord your God with all your heart.' . . . This is the first and greatest commandment. And the second is like it: 'Love your neighbor as yourself.' All the Law and Prophets hang on these two commandments" (Matthew 22:37–40). When we experience a breakdown in our relationship with God, a breakdown in our relationship with people follows. The connection between the two is unbreakable.

Jesus also linked our ability to love people with our ability to bear witness to him in the world: "Everyone will know you are my

11

disciples, if you love one another" (John 13:35). In other words, when we don't love well, the implications go beyond our personal lives, our families, our neighborhoods, and our churches. When we don't love others well, the beauty and love of Jesus is tarnished and sullied to the world.

So it is critically important that we grow as Christ followers in our ability to love people. That is the purpose behind *The Emotionally Healthy (EH) Relationships Course*, which teaches eight core relationship skills that equip us to love others in a mature way. Yet, this is not enough. We must also mature in our relationship with Jesus, opening our human relationships to him so he can reshape them as he reshapes us. That is the reason this devotional guide is developed from and anchored to the eight foundational skills of *The EH Relationships Course*.[1]

Sadly, too many of us have a relationship with Jesus that is seriously underdeveloped. We talk *to* God, or even perhaps *at* God, but we don't actually listen to him very much. And that is nothing less than a spiritual crisis.

But what if I told you that, while the problem is real and pervasive, it is far from a lost cause? There *is* a way to live a relaxed, unhurried, contented life in Jesus amid the pressures and difficulties of life. There *is* a way to mature into spiritual adulthood anchored in the love of God. There *is* a way to remain thoughtful when triggered in conversations, and to listen for God's voice in those experiences. There *is* a way to surrender to God's love and will when we are tempted to lash out or be judgmental—even when it is difficult. There *is* a way to give our lives in service to others without becoming chronically exhausted. How are all these things possible? The answer lies in intentionally rearranging our days to routinely integrate the Christian practice of being still and silent in God's presence.

AN ANCIENT AND REVOLUTIONARY SPIRITUAL DISCIPLINE

The purpose of this book is to introduce you to this spiritual discipline that is both ancient and revolutionary. It's called the "Daily Office."[2] The Daily Office provides a structured way of spending time with God each day, but it differs from what we tend to think of as "quiet time" or "devotions." Quiet time and devotions normally take place once a day, usually in the morning, and focus on "getting filled up" for the day or on interceding for the needs of others. The Daily Office takes place at least twice a day, and is not so much about turning to God to *get* something as it is turning to God to simply *be with* him.

The goal of the Daily Office is to pay attention to God throughout the entire day—*in the midst of our activities*. This is the great challenge for all of us. The enormous pressure of the world and our own stubborn self-will make it extraordinarily difficult to sustain any consistent awareness of God's presence. But it is far from impossible.

So why is it called the "Daily Office"? The word *office* comes from the Latin word *opus*, or "work." For the early church, the Daily Office—praying at fixed times throughout the day—was always the first "work of God" to be done. Nothing was to interfere with that priority.

But this practice of fixed-hour prayer is one that actually long predates the early church. Three thousand years ago, King David practiced set times of prayer seven times a day (Psalm 119:164). The prophet Daniel prayed three times a day (Daniel 6:10). Devout Jews in Jesus' time prayed at morning, afternoon, and evening. Such set times of prayer were one of the Israelites' great spiritual and cultural treasures, a practical way to keep their lives centered on loving God at all times. Even after the resurrection, Jesus' disciples continued to pray at certain hours of the day (Acts 3:1; 10:2–23).

It was about AD 525 when a monk named Benedict created a formal structure for these prayer times that he anchored in eight Daily Offices (including one for monks in the middle of the night). Prayer was the framework for the day, and everything else in their lives was ordered around it. Benedict wrote: "On hearing the signal for an hour of the divine office, the monk will immediately set aside what he has in hand and go with utmost speed. Indeed, nothing is to be preferred to the Work of God [the Daily Office]."[3]

All of these people—from the ancient Israelites to first-century disciples and early Christian leaders like Benedict—realized that stopping to be with God, by means of the Daily Office, was the key to creating a continual and easy familiarity with God's presence. And having practiced the Daily Office for over fifteen years, I can affirm it has done that for me. Routinely setting aside small units of time for morning, midday, and evening prayer infuses the activities of my day with a deep awareness of the sacred—of God. In those moments, I remember that all time is God's time. There is no division between the sacred and the secular.

HOW TO USE THIS BOOK

Emotionally Healthy Relationships Day by Day provides a flexible structure for your time with God. My hope is that you will adapt it to the unique needs and demands of this season in your life. God has built each of us differently. What works for one person will not necessarily work for another, and what worked for you at one time in the past may no longer work for you now. Allow grace—not legalism—to be the foundation for your practice.

The book includes material to guide you through a forty-day journey of praying the Daily Office. I've collected the days into eight weekly themes, each one based on a session theme from *The EH Relationships Course*:[4]

Week One: Take Your Community Temperature Reading
Week Two: Stop Mind Reading and Clarify Expectations
Week Three: Genogram Your Family
Week Four: Explore the Iceberg
Week Five: Listen Incarnationally
Week Six: Climb the Ladder of Integrity
Week Seven: Fight Cleanly
Week Eight: Develop a Rule of Life to Implement
    Emotionally Healthy Skills

These skills, or tools, have been developed, refined, and lived out for more than twenty-one years at New Life Fellowship Church. They are designed to help ordinary people in diverse contexts to unlock and live out Scripture's command to love well in our homes, churches, workplaces, schools, and neighborhoods. The goal is to grow us into emotionally mature adults who love others so distinctly that they know Jesus is truly alive and present in their midst. As previously noted, the Offices in this devotional supplement the content of *The EH Relationships Course* (which also includes a DVD and workbook) and provide a means to stay deeply connected to Jesus, who reminds us: "Apart from me you can do nothing" (John 15:5b). On the last page of the devotional you will find a checklist to keep you on track as you move through the Course. Fill it out along the way and, when completed, go to emotionallyhealthy.org to receive your certificate of completion.

There are two Offices per day—one for morning or midday, and the other for midday or evening. You may, for example, do one in the morning and the other at midday, or one at midday and the other in the evening before you go to bed. You choose the length of time for your Offices. The key, however, is to keep your focus on attending to God, not the number of minutes you spend with God. Pausing to be with God might last anywhere from two to twenty to forty-five minutes. My wife, Geri, and I choose to have longer times with God in the mornings and then shorter ones at midday and in the evenings. It is up to you.

Each Office contains five elements: Silence and Stillness, Scripture, Devotional, Question to Consider, and Prayer.

1. Silence and Stillness

This is the foundation of a Daily Office. We stop our activity and turn our attention to the Living God. We heed the words of the psalmist: "Be still before the LORD and wait patiently for him" (Psalm 37:7), and "Be still, and know that I am God" (Psalm 46:10). We choose to enter into awareness of God's presence and to rest there in his love. That choice alone is no small feat. There are occasions when I pause for my midday prayer and find that I spend the entire time—be it five or twenty minutes—centering my thoughts so I can let go of tensions and distractions and begin resting in the love of God.

Each Office begins and ends with two minutes of silence and stillness. Many religions have some practice of silence, so there is nothing particularly Christian about the silence itself. What makes silence unique for us as followers of Christ is that we are still and silent in the context of our relationship with the living God. In a posture of attentiveness and surrender, we allow him and his will access to the innermost parts of our lives. This is the very core of what it means to be in loving union with him.[5]

This may be difficult for you, especially at first. Our internal and external worlds are filled with noise and distractions. For this reason, spending time alone with God in silence is perhaps the most challenging and least experienced spiritual practice among Christians today. However, that doesn't justify taking a pass. If we fail to learn how to be quiet in God's presence—to stop talking long enough and routinely enough to listen—how will we ever mature into Christian adults? How will our relationship with God develop any depth?

There are a number of ways to approach this. The following are a few guidelines to help you begin entering into silence and stillness:[6]

- Settle into a comfortable and quiet place. Take a few deep breaths, allowing yourself to inhale and exhale slowly. (For additional guidance on a practice called the "breath prayer," see Appendix B.)
- Begin with a simple prayer—often just one word—that expresses your openness to God and your desire to spend time with him. You might use your favorite name for God, such as *Abba, Father,* or *Jesus.* Or you could use a phrase such as, *Here I am, Lord.* (My wife, Geri, often doesn't use any words, preferring to spend time with Jesus as two lovers might, content to simply be together in a quiet corner. In those moments, she imagines God wrapping his arms of love around her.)
- When distractions come—and they most certainly will come—entrust them to God's care and use your simple prayer phrase to turn your thoughts back to God.

Give yourself lots of grace here, especially at the beginning. Remember, this is a revolutionary and countercultural practice, not a walk in the park. When you choose to sit in silence and stillness, you are choosing to allow God to be the center of your life. That means you are choosing, even if just for a few moments, to let go of control and your own agenda.

That is no small thing.

If you persevere through the awkwardness at the beginning—if you truly stop to surrender your will to God's will—you will begin to experience a gradual transformation. And slowly, you will find that silence will become a normal and regular part of each day. You will find yourself briefly pausing for silence, for example, before turning on the car, writing a difficult email, or starting a meeting at work. Before you begin, you may find it helpful to read through Appendix C: *Top Ten FAQs about Practicing Silence.*

2. Scripture

The important thing to remember here is the adage that "less is more." The Scripture selections are intentionally brief. Read slowly—possibly aloud—chewing on any words or phrases that stand out to you. If God leads you to linger over a verse, do so. Be attentive to what God is doing inside you. There is no need to finish all that is provided for each office! Allow the Holy Spirit to guide you.

3. Devotional

Readings are drawn from a wide variety of sources—ancient spiritual writers, poets, monks, rabbis, and contemporary writers, as well as some of my own writings. As with Scripture, these selections are meant to be read slowly and prayerfully. There are times when I come to the midday or evening office with so much on my mind that I actually choose to begin my time of silence with the devotional reading as a means of redirecting my thoughts to God. Sometimes the readings will speak powerfully to where you are. At other times, you may find yourself wanting to skim or skip them. Once again, it's important to remember that the purpose of the Daily Office is to commune with God, not to get through all the reading!

4. Question to Consider

Each office ends with a brief but probing question. You may find it helpful to write out your answers in the form of a prayer to God. Or, if you don't find the questions helpful, feel free to skip them. If you use this guide repeatedly over time, don't be surprised if God leads you along very different paths as you reflect on the questions each time.

5. Prayer

For a large part of my Christian life, I avoided written prayers. In recent years, however, I have found them to be a rich supplement to my devotional life. You may want to pray the words as written, or simply use them as inspiration and a starting point for your own prayers. Note that The Lord's Prayer is included in Appendix A as an additional resource for your time with God. Because of its depth and simplicity, I often pray it as part of my Daily Offices each day. Again, use these prayers only if you find them helpful.

In Appendix D, I have also included instructions about compline (pronounced "comp-line" or "comp-lin"), which is a going-to-sleep prayer of trust. Although it is prayed at the end of the day, I find that it also helps me to pay attention to God during all my waking hours.

USING THE DAILY OFFICE WITH GROUPS

The Daily Offices are written for individuals but they can be easily adapted for groups meeting for morning, midday, or evening prayer. Here are a few guidelines:

- Appoint a facilitator to pace the time.
- Read the Scripture selections aloud together.
- Appoint one person to read aloud the Devotional and the Question to Consider.
- Pause briefly—five to ten seconds—between each section of the Office.
- **Option:** When our staff at New Life meets for midday prayer, rather than read the closing prayer aloud together at the end, we break up into groups of two or three for intercession, and then close with a worship song. Be flexible for what works best in your context.

CLOSING THOUGHTS

As you begin your journey with the Daily Office, I encourage you to allow yourself a lot of time and practice to make progress. Few of us have life-giving rhythms, so rearranging our days to stop and be with Jesus is a major shift. Add to this the reality that little silence exists in the culture, our families of origin, even in our churches, and the challenge can feel overwhelming. But I can assure you that if you will persevere and ask the Holy Spirit for help, you will find that God has been waiting for you. You will get to know him in ways that can happen only in silence (Psalm 46:10). Your listening-to-God "muscles" may develop slowly, but they will develop. By God's grace, your capacity to be with Jesus will enlarge and expand. Your relationships will change, with more of Jesus flowing out of you and less of the bad patterns you may have learned from the culture or your family of origin. But most importantly, you will discover, as millions of others have across the ages, that his love really is better than life (Psalm 63:3).

Take Your
Community
Temperature Reading

One of the most loving, God-glorifying things we can do in our relationships is to speak in healthy, loving ways. In fact, part of the reason God gives us the gift of words is to express ourselves and to nurture life-giving relationships. Nevertheless, our relationships often stagnate or suffer because we are unsure of how to do that in practical ways.

When we use the skill called Take Your Community Temperature Reading, we are intentional about utilizing words to express ourselves and nurture relationships in practical ways, such as speaking appreciations, sharing hopes and dreams, and stating complaints maturely. This is how we take our first steps in integrating a growing love for God with a growing love for others and ourselves.

ADDITIONAL RESOURCES

The Daily Offices throughout this book were written to be used in companionship with *The Emotionally Healthy (EH) Relationships Course*. Each week, the corresponding session from the course and the DVD are listed as additional resources.

- *The Emotionally Healthy Relationships Workbook*, Session 1
- *The Emotionally Healthy Relationships* DVD, Session 1

DAY 1 MORNING/MIDDAY OFFICE

Silence and Stillness before God (2 minutes)

Scripture Reading: John 15:4–5, 8–9, 12

Remain in me, as I also remain in you. No branch can bear
fruit by itself; it must remain in the vine. Neither can you
bear fruit unless you remain in me. I am the vine; you are
the branches. If you remain in me and I in you, you will bear
much fruit; apart from me you can do nothing. . . . This
is to my Father's glory, that you bear much fruit, showing
yourselves to be my disciples. As the Father has loved me, so
have I loved you. Now remain in my love. . . . My command
is this: Love each other as I have loved you.

Devotional

Loving well is the essence of true spirituality. It requires experiencing connection with God, with others, and with oneself.
It begins, however, with our response to God's invitation
to practice his presence in our daily lives. He then invites
us to "practice the presence of people" within an awareness
of his presence. But learning to practice his presence is no
small task.

There is perhaps no greater teacher to offer us insight on how
to do this than Brother Lawrence, an obscure, sixteenth-century
Carmelite monk from Paris. He resolved to live in continual
awareness of God's presence, to never forget him from one

moment to the next. In fact, he defined prayer as simply cultivating an awareness of the presence of God.

These words from Brother Lawrence have served me well over
the years, helping me to remain in Jesus when I am distracted:

> The time of business . . . does not differ from the time of
> prayer; and in the noise and clatter of the kitchen, while
> several persons are at the same time calling for different
> things, I possess God in as great tranquility as if I were
> upon my knees. . . .
>
> I make it my business only to persevere in his holy pres-
> ence . . . which I may call an actual presence of God; or, to
> speak better, an habitual, silent and secret conversation of
> the soul with God.[7]

Jesus said it simply: If we remain in him, allowing ourselves
to be held in his embrace, his life will flow out of us to others. If
we choose not to remain in him, we will have little, if anything,
to offer others.

Question to Consider

When can you set aside uninterrupted time each day to begin
cultivating an awareness of the presence of God?

Prayer

*Lord, it is so easy for me to go through my days without remem-
bering or thinking about you. And it is even easier for me to*

overlook your beauty in the people around me. Please change
the unhealthy ways of relating that are so deeply rooted in me.
Shape me into a person who offers your tenderness and kindness
to those I come in contact with today. In Jesus' name, amen.

Conclude with Silence (2 minutes)

DAY 1 MIDDAY/EVENING OFFICE

Silence and Stillness before God (2 minutes)

Scripture Reading: Romans 7:18b–21, 24–45

For I have the desire to do what is good, but I cannot carry it
out. For I do not do the good I want to do, but the evil I do
not want to do—this I keep on doing. Now if I do what I do
not want to do, it is no longer I who do it, but it is sin living
in me that does it. So I find this law at work: Although I
want to do good, evil is right there with me. . . . What a
wretched man I am! Who will rescue me from this body
that is subject to death? Thanks be to God, who delivers
me through Jesus Christ our Lord!

Devotional

Jean Vanier is the founder of L'Arche, an international network
of 147 communities in thirty-five countries, for persons with
mental and physical disabilities. While Vanier was visiting
France in 1963, he had his first encounter with men living in

government-sponsored psychiatric hospitals, and he quickly understood them to be "the most oppressed people on the planet." The first L'Arche community began a few months later when he invited two men, Raphael Simi and Philippe Seux, to leave their institution and live with him in a small village north of Paris. His insights about our task and difficulty to love well are powerful:

> Living with men and women with mental disabilities has helped me to discover what it means to live in communion with someone. To be in communion means to be with someone . . . accepting people just as they are, with all their limits and inner pain, but also with their gifts and their beauty . . . to see the beauty inside of all the pain. To love someone is not first of all to do things for them, but to reveal to them their beauty and value, to say to them through our attitude: "You are beautiful. You are important. I trust you. You can trust yourself. . . ."
>
> Communion did not come easily to me. . . . As I began living with people like Raphael and Philip, I began to see the hardness of my heart. . . . Raphael and the others were crying out simply for friendship and I did not quite know how to respond because of the other forces within me, pulling me to go up the ladder. . . . They have been teaching me that behind the need for me to win, there are my own fears and anguish, the fear of being devalued or pushed aside, the fear of opening up my heart and of being vulnerable or of

feeling helpless in front of others in pain; there is the pain and brokenness of my own heart.

I discovered something which I had never confronted before, that there were immense forces of darkness and hatred within my own heart.[8]

Vanier's journey to grow in love forced him to confront the evil and hardness within his own heart. Nonetheless, out of his brokenness, God met him and taught him that love is more than simply doing things for people; it is revealing "to them their beauty and value." May God meet you and teach you this same powerful truth as you seek to love others this day.

Question to Consider

Whose beauty might you be bypassing because you are too busy or distracted?

Prayer

Lord, when I consider that love is revealing to others their beauty and value, the hardness of my heart reveals itself. Forgive and cleanse me. Help me to truly love others, to say to them through my attitude, "You are beautiful. You are important. I trust you. You can trust yourself." Please make me like you so I might love those around me the way you do. In Jesus' name, amen.

Conclude with Silence (2 minutes)

DAY 2 MORNING/MIDDAY OFFICE

Silence and Stillness before God (2 minutes)

Scripture Reading: Luke 15:20b–32

But while he [the younger brother] was still a long way off, his father saw him and was filled with compassion for him; he ran to his son, threw his arms around him and kissed him.... The father said to his servants, "Quick! Bring the best robe and put it on him. Put a ring on his finger and sandals on his feet. Bring the fattened calf and kill it. Let's have a feast and celebrate...."

Meanwhile, the older son was in the field. When he came near the house, he heard music and dancing. So he called one of the servants and asked him what was going on. "Your brother has come," he replied, "and your father has killed the fattened calf because he has him back safe and sound."

The older brother became angry and refused to go in. So his father went out and pleaded with him. But he answered his father, "Look! All these years I've been slaving for you and never disobeyed your orders. Yet you never gave me even a young goat so I could celebrate with my friends. But when this son of yours who has squandered your property with prostitutes comes home, you kill the fattened calf for him!"

"My son," the father said, "you are always with me, and everything I have is yours. But we had to celebrate and be glad, because this brother of yours was dead and is alive again; he was lost and is found."

Devotional

In the parable of the Prodigal Son, we learn that whenever we wander from the love of the Father, we are lost. We see this in the younger son who rebelled against his father and ran away from home. We also see it in the elder brother who remained obedient to the Father but was equally lost. He too had wandered from the love of the Father. As Henri Nouwen has written:

> The lostness of the elder son . . . is much harder to identify. After all, he did all the right things. He was obedient, dutiful, law-abiding, and hardworking. . . . Outwardly, the elder son was faultless. But when confronted by his father's joy at the return of his younger brother, a dark power erupts in him and boils to the surface. . . .
>
> There are many elder sons and elder daughters who are lost while still at home. And it is this lostness— characterized by judgment and condemnation, anger and resentment, bitterness and jealousy—that is so pernicious and damaging to the human heart. . . . There is so much frozen anger among the people who are so concerned about avoiding "sin." . . .
>
> I recognize the elder son in me. Often I catch myself complaining about little rejections, little impolitenesses, little negligences. Time and again I discover within me that murmuring, whining, grumbling, lamenting, and griping that go on and on even against my will.[9]

Jesus' parable of the Prodigal Son reminds us how quickly and easily we can become the elder brother—bitter, judgmental, grumbling, jealous, and proud. It also offers one of the most vivid pictures in Scripture of the love of God, a love that invites us to turn to him over and over again, all day and every day.

Question to Consider

In what areas of life might your pursuit of "getting things done" or "doing right things" be more important to you than seeking a loving relationship with God and others?

Prayer

Father, it is so easy for me to get lost in anger, resentment, or jealousy of others, and fail to hear your voice of love calling me home. Melt away my resentments and unforgiveness toward others with your love. And free me to love others with your love. In Jesus' name, amen.

Conclude with Silence (2 minutes)

DAY 2 MIDDAY/EVENING OFFICE

Silence and Stillness before God (2 minutes)

Scripture Reading: Luke 4:42–44; 5:15

At daybreak, Jesus went out to a solitary place. The people were looking for him and when they came to where he was, they tried to keep him from leaving them. But he said, "I must proclaim the good news of the kingdom of God to the other towns also, because that is why I was sent." And he kept on preaching in the synagogues of Judea. . . .

Yet the news about him spread all the more, so that crowds of people came to hear him and to be healed of their sicknesses. But Jesus often withdrew to lonely places and prayed.

Devotional

On April 9, 1945, German pastor and theologian Dietrich Bonhoeffer was executed for his resistance to Hitler's Nazi regime. During his years of resistance, he penned these famous words in his book *Life Together*:

> *Whoever cannot be alone should beware of community.* Such people will only do harm to themselves and to the community. Alone you stood before God when God called you. Alone you had to obey God's voice. Alone you had to take up your cross, had to struggle and pray, and alone you will die and give an account to God. You cannot avoid yourself; for it is precisely God has singled you out. . . .
>
> But the reverse is also true: *Whoever cannot stand being in community should beware of being alone.* You are called into the community of faith; the call was not meant for you alone. . . . You are not alone, even when you die. . . . If you neglect the community of other Christians, you reject the

call of Jesus Christ, and thus your being alone can only be
harmful for you.[10]

Bonhoeffer warns us that when we do not take time to be
alone in God's presence, we become dangerous or harmful
to others. We may demand people meet our needs for love,
approval, and self-worth—a weight too heavy for them to
bear. We may feed off others in inappropriate ways and cause
damage. We need people, but they can never fully fill us with
the perfect love that can only be given by God. For this reason,
it is vital that we consistently practice silence and stillness
with God.

Question to Consider

Consider your present balance between solitude and community.
To what degree is it adequate for you to be growing in love for
God, others, and yourself?

Prayer

*Lord, I confess to you that I am not sure I can discern the
appropriate balance of solitude and community at this junc-
ture of my life. I ask you to lead me on this journey. Help
me to be intentional in pursuing both stillness with you and
engagement in healthy community with others. I ask this in
Jesus' name, amen.*

Conclude with Silence (2 minutes)

DAY 3 MORNING/MIDDAY OFFICE

Silence and Stillness before God (2 minutes)

Scripture Reading: 1 John 4:10, 15–16, 18a

This is love: not that we loved God, but that he loved us and sent his Son as an atoning sacrifice for our sins. . . . If anyone acknowledges that Jesus is the Son of God, God lives in them and they in God. And so we know and rely on the love God has for us.

God is love. Whoever lives in love lives in God, and God in them. . . . There is no fear in love. But perfect love drives out fear.

Devotional

For the apostle John, learning to live in the immensity of the love of God is the power and source from which we love others. God's love is always first. Søren Kierkegaard, a Danish philosopher and theologian (1813–1855), summed it up well:

You have loved us first, O God, alas! We speak of it in terms of history as if You loved us first but a single time, rather than that without ceasing You have loved us first many times and every day and our whole life through. When we wake up in the morning and turn our soul toward You— You are there first—You have loved us first; if I rise at dawn and at that same second turn my soul toward You in prayer,

You are there ahead of me, You have loved me first. When I withdraw from the distractions of the day and turn my soul toward You, You are there first and thus forever. And we speak ungratefully as if You have loved us first only once.[11]

Kierkegaard captures for us a glimpse of the extraordinary nature of the love of God. So often we think we are waiting on God when the truth is that he is waiting on us. God is more different from us than the human mind is capable of grasping. His love is without strings and without conditions. He simply loves human beings, and there is nothing we can do, or not do, that will change that love. We will spend eternity in awe and wonder of this love that surpasses knowledge, a love so great that God became a human being in Jesus to die for our sins.

Question to Consider

What difference might it make in your day to remember that, in every moment you turn your heart to God—including this very moment—he is waiting for you and loving you first?

Prayer

Lord, open up and expand the container of my heart to receive the depth and breadth of your love that surpasses knowledge and flows toward me every moment of every day. And may your love then flow through me to those around me today. In Jesus' name, amen.

Conclude with Silence (2 minutes)

DAY 3 MIDDAY/EVENING OFFICE

Silence and Stillness before God (2 minutes)

Scripture Reading: Luke 10:38–42

> As Jesus and his disciples were on their way, he came to a
> village where a woman named Martha opened her home to
> him. She had a sister called Mary, who sat at the Lord's feet
> listening to what he said. But Martha was distracted by all
> the preparations that had to be made. She came to him and
> asked, "Lord, don't you care that my sister has left me to do
> the work by myself? Tell her to help me!"
>
> "Martha, Martha," the Lord answered, "you are worried
> and upset about many things, but few things are needed—or
> indeed only one. Mary has chosen what is better, and it will
> not be taken away from her."

Devotional

This familiar story of Martha and Mary teaches us why it is essential
to slow down to sit at the feet of Jesus if we are to love others well.

Martha is completely caught up in the demands of preparing
an important meal for some very distinguished guests: Jesus and
his twelve disciples. Among other things, her to-do list includes
shopping for ingredients; setting a large table; prepping food;
borrowing additional mats, tables, and serving plates from
neighbors; cleaning the house; serving the meal; and perhaps
most importantly, making sure everything goes perfectly.

But Martha is resentful, especially at her sister Mary, who sits idly by enjoying the company of Jesus. Martha is too distracted and irritated to enjoy her guests or Jesus. In trying to accomplish too much, she not only loses sight of herself but of the very purpose of all her hard work—to welcome and care for her guests, including Christ himself.

Question to Consider

Think back over the last few days. In what way(s) did your to-do list, distractibility, or perfectionism keep you from loving and enjoying Jesus or the people around you?

Prayer

> *Lord, help me to honor my own boundaries and limits in doing for others so that I don't become resentful. And teach me to slow down, stop, and sit at your feet in stillness that I might love others in ways that reflect you. In Jesus' name, amen.*

Conclude with Silence (2 minutes)

DAY 4 MORNING/MIDDAY OFFICE

Silence and Stillness before God (2 minutes)

Scripture Reading: Matthew 7:1–5

> Do not judge, or you too will be judged. For in the same way you judge others, you will be judged, and with the measure you use, it will be measured to you.

Why do you look at the speck of sawdust in your brother's
eye and pay no attention to the plank in your own eye? How
can you say to your brother, "Let me take the speck out of your
eye," when all the time there is a plank in your own eye? You
hypocrite, first take the plank out of your own eye, and then
you will see clearly to remove the speck from your brother's eye.

Devotional

A synonym for the word *judge* is *despise*. It happens when we
harden our heart toward someone. In the context of Matthew 7,
the issue with judgment is not discernment of good and evil,
right or wrong, but the condemnation of "writing someone off."

Anthony the Great (254–356 AD) is perhaps the earliest
and most significant teacher among the Christian desert fathers.
He wrote:

> Our life and our death is with our neighbor. If we win our
> brother, we win God. If we cause our brother to stumble,
> we have sinned against Christ.[12]

When Anthony refers to death with our neighbor, he means
that we renounce our right to pronounce judgment over them—a
challenge difficult enough to be described as a death.

Theodore of Pherme, another prominent fourth-century
desert father, went so far as to say that a mature, nonjudgmental
love toward others is the foundational virtue or character quality
upon which all others are built:

There is no other virtue than that of not being scornful [despising anyone].[13]

Maximus the Confessor (580–662 AD), a Christian theologian, monk, and advisor to the emperor of Constantinople, captured this truth through another lens:

Interior freedom is not possessed by anyone who cannot close his eyes to the fault of a friend, whether real or apparent.[14]

The early desert fathers understood that it is impossible to think about the spiritual life apart from living in loving community with others. They emphasized that genuine spirituality is marked by a humility that seeks to hide the faults of others rather than expose them, and that the nearer we draw to God in love, the nearer we are drawn in love to our neighbor. They understood that when we harden our hearts to another person, we harden our hearts to Christ.

Question to Consider

In what subtle or perhaps even unconscious ways might you be judging or despising someone in your life?

Prayer

Father, I fear that my tendency to look down on and judge others is so much a part of me that I scarcely notice it. Grant

me an awareness, by the Holy Spirit, of when my tone of
voice, facial expressions, words, or actions fail to communicate
safety, acceptance, or tenderness to those around me. In Jesus'
name, amen.

Conclude with Silence (2 minutes)

DAY 4 MIDDAY/EVENING OFFICE

Silence and Stillness before God (2 minutes)

Scripture Reading: Mark 14:3–6

While he [Jesus] was in Bethany, reclining at the table in the
home of Simon the Leper, a woman came with an alabaster
jar of very expensive perfume, made of pure nard. She broke
the jar and poured the perfume on his head.

Some of those present were saying indignantly to one
another, "Why this waste of perfume? It could have been
sold for more than a year's wages and the money given to
the poor." And they rebuked her harshly.

"Leave her alone," said Jesus. "Why are you bothering
her? She has done a beautiful thing to me."

Devotional

Pedro Arrupe (1907–1991) left medical school and a promising career to join the Jesuits in 1927, but in 1945 his medical
training was put to use when he led the first rescue team into

Hiroshima, Japan, after the atomic bomb was dropped on that city. He offers us insight into the power of the love of Jesus to transform all we do:

> Nothing is more practical than finding God, than falling in love in a quite absolute, final way. What you are in love with, what seizes your imagination, will affect everything. It will decide what will get you out of bed in the morning, what you will do with your evenings, how you spend your weekends, what you read, whom you know, what breaks your heart, and what amazes you with joy and gratitude. Fall in love, stay in love, and it will decide everything.[15]

The woman who anointed Jesus with the alabaster jar of perfume was not preoccupied with what others thought of her. Christ's love and forgiveness had, in Arrupe's words, already "decided everything." Her heart brimmed over with thankfulness to Jesus for his love and mercy. She understood that her significance came from her relationship to Jesus, not from the approval of others. This gave her confidence to be herself, regardless of what others might think about her.

Question to Consider

In your own life, how might it be true that falling in love with Jesus and staying in love with Jesus will decide everything? How could it change you, as well as your relationships?

Prayer

> *I arise today through the strength of heaven;*
> *Light of sun, radiance of moon,*
> *Splendor of fire, speed of lightning,*
> *Swiftness of wind, depth of sea,*
> *Stability of earth, firmness of rock.*
> *I arise today through God's strength to pilot me . . .*
> *God's word to speak for me,*
> *God's hand to guard me,*
> *God's way to lie before me . . .*
> *I summon today all these powers between me and evil,*
> *Against every cruel, merciless power that*
> *may oppose my body and soul.*

—Attributed to Saint Patrick, 500 AD

Conclude with Silence (2 minutes)

DAY 5 MORNING/MIDDAY OFFICE

Silence and Stillness before God (2 minutes)

Scripture Reading: Luke 17:11–19

Now on his way to Jerusalem, Jesus traveled along the border between Samaria and Galilee. As he was going into a village, ten men who had leprosy met him. They stood at a distance and called out in a loud voice, "Jesus, Master, have pity on us!"

When he saw them, he said, "Go, show yourselves to the priests." And as they went, they were cleansed.

One of them, when he saw he was healed, came back, praising God in a loud voice. He threw himself at Jesus' feet and thanked him—and he was a Samaritan.

Jesus asked, "Were not all ten cleansed? Where are the other nine? Has no one returned to give praise to God except this foreigner?" Then he said to him, "Rise and go; your faith has made you well."

Devotional

God repeatedly invites us to cultivate gratitude—not just with an occasional prayer, but as a way of life. Consider just a few of the psalmists' many commands to be thankful:

Give thanks to the LORD, for he is good. (Psalm 107:1)

Sacrifice thank offerings to God. . . . Those who sacrifice thank offerings honor me. (Psalm 50:14, 23)

Let us come before him with thanksgiving. (Psalm 95:2)

The problem is that we so easily take things for granted. At times, we even feel entitled. We expect, and sometimes even demand, that things in life go our way. Yet God invites us to give thanks for the big and small gifts that come into our lives each day. Why? We all depend—in every detail and moment of life—on him.

"Blessed is he who expects nothing," said Francis of Assisi, "for he shall enjoy everything." Francis understood that none of us can earn the beauty of a star in the sky or a sunset on the horizon, that our utter dependence on God is the very rock of reality. Irish poet and author John O'Donohue put it this way: "Because we are so engaged with the world, we usually forget how fragile life can be and how vulnerable we always are. It takes only a couple of seconds for a life to change irreversibly."[16]

One of the great wonders of life is that, when we make gratitude—expressing appreciations—a way of life, God changes not only us but also our relationships and the communities in which we participate, including family, friends, neighbors, colleagues, and brothers and sisters in Christ.

Question to Consider

What two or three things from the past week are you most thankful for? (For example, good health or healing, people in your life, possessions, opportunities, trials, closed doors, spiritual blessings, etc.) Express your heartfelt gratitude to God for these gifts.

Prayer

Father, it is easy for me to walk around with a sense of entitlement and forget how fragile life is, how everything is a gift. Even as I live in a culture of striving and anxiety, teach me gratefulness and contentment—in everything and for everything. In Jesus' name, amen.

Conclude with Silence (2 minutes)

DAY 5 MIDDAY/EVENING OFFICE

Silence and Stillness before God (2 minutes)

Scripture Reading: Genesis 4:2–8

Now Abel kept flocks, and Cain worked the soil. In the course of time Cain brought some of the fruits of the soil as an offering to the LORD. And Abel also brought an offering—fat portions from some of the firstborn of his flock. The LORD looked with favor on Abel and his offering, but on Cain and his offering he did not look with favor. So Cain was very angry, and his face was downcast.

Then the LORD said to Cain, "Why are you angry? Why is your face downcast? If you do what is right, will you not be accepted? But if you do not do what is right, sin is crouching at your door; it desires to have you, but you must rule over it."

Now Cain said to his brother Abel, "Let's go out to the field." While they were in the field, Cain attacked his brother Abel and killed him.

Devotional

The story of Cain and Abel illustrates our need to grow in love for God and for our neighbor at the same time. Cain's broken relationship with God leads to a broken relationship with his brother Abel.

Jesus summarized the entire Bible in one simple, powerful truth:

> "Love the Lord your God with all your heart and with all your soul and with all your mind." This is the first and greatest commandment. And the second is like it: "Love your neighbor as yourself." All the Law and the Prophets hang on these two commandments. (Matthew 22:37–40)

Five hundred years later, monk and abbot Dorotheus of Gaza pointed out that, much like the spokes in a wheel—which are separate but meet at the center—the closer we draw to God in love, the more we will be united to our neighbor.

In the sixteenth century, Teresa of Avila wrote:

> There are only two duties that our Lord requires of us: the love of God, and the love of our neighbor. And, in my opinion, the surest sign for our discovering our love to God is discovering our love to our neighbor. Be assured that the further you advance in the love of your neighbor, the more you are advancing in the love of God.[17]

The temptation to separate our love for God from our love for a neighbor has been with us since the beginning of time. But as Jesus taught, *the heart of genuine spirituality is love of God and others.*

Question to Consider

What is your biggest challenge in integrating these two loves in this season of your life?

Prayer

Father, I find it so much easier to be with you than to deal with tensions and conflicts in my relationships with other human beings. I open the door of my heart to you, fully and wide. Fill me with the Holy Spirit and help me to grow today into an emotionally mature adult who loves well. In Jesus' name, amen.

Conclude with Silence (2 minutes)

Stop Mind Reading and Clarify Expectations

Stop Mind Reading and Clarify Expectations are two practical tools, or skills, that help to eliminate misunderstandings and assumptions that wreak havoc in relationships. Because of unmet expectations, marriages end, churches split, employees quit, and families fragment. If we are to respect and love others as Jesus did, it is essential to refrain from assuming we know what others are thinking. Moreover, we must guard against harboring unspoken, unconscious, unrealistic, or un-agreed upon expectations of others.

Spending time with God each week through the Daily Office helps us surrender our will and plans to him, recognizing we need Jesus' love in us if it is to flow out of us.

ADDITIONAL RESOURCES

- *The Emotionally Healthy Relationships Workbook*, Session 2
- *The Emotionally Healthy Relationships DVD*, Session 2

DAY 1 MORNING/MIDDAY OFFICE

Silence and Stillness before God (2 minutes)

Scripture Reading: 1 Thessalonians 5:14–18

And we urge you, brothers and sisters, warn those who are idle and disruptive, encourage the disheartened, help the weak, be patient with everyone. Make sure that nobody pays back wrong for wrong, but always strive to do what is good for each other and for everyone else.

Rejoice always, pray continually, give thanks in all circumstances; for this is God's will for you in Christ Jesus.

Devotional

At the age of fifteen, Marie Françoise-Thérèse Martin obtained special permission to enter a Carmelite monastic community in Lisieux, a small town in northwestern France. We know her today as Thérèse of Lisieux. Although she died at age twenty-four, theologians have spent a century commenting on the depth and originality of her spiritual insights.

Her focus on loving and serving God in the ordinary circumstances of life became known as the "little way." It grew out of Jesus' command: "Let the little children come to me, and do not hinder them, for the kingdom of heaven belongs to such as these" (Matthew 19:14). Thérèse was convinced that Jesus wanted us to live lives of great love that came from a childlike trust in God. She did this by offering God small, everyday acts of love: going out of her way to befriend the crankiest nun in the convent; refusing to complain when accused of a wrong she didn't commit; choosing to cheerfully and silently endure a cold bedroom, an insult, or another nun's tendency of splashing dirty water on her when they did laundry together.[18]

> But I want to seek . . . a little way that is very straight, very short, a completely new little way. . . . My mortifications [putting to death her flesh] consisted in breaking my will, which was always ready to impose itself; in holding my tongue instead of answering back; in doing little things for others without hoping to get anything in return.[19]

> This is how my life will be consumed. . . . strewing flowers, that is, not allowing one sacrifice to escape, not one look, one word, profiting by all the smallest things and doing them through love.[20]

Thérèse of Lisieux offered up these slights and sufferings as flowers to her heavenly Father, recognizing them as opportunities for her to express her love for God.

Question to Consider

How might you follow a "little way" of love today in a situation where you might otherwise express annoyance, impatience, or frustration?

Prayer

Father, this is challenging, very challenging. Viewing people as annoyances, interruptions, or even the enemy is a large part of how I behave each day. I ask you to heal and deliver me that I might see difficult people as a means of grace that you can use to break my will and transform me into a gentle, kind, and loving person. In Jesus' name, amen.

Conclude with Silence (2 minutes)

DAY 1 MIDDAY/EVENING OFFICE

Silence and Stillness before God (2 minutes)

Scripture Reading

The wisdom of the prudent is to give thought to their ways. (Proverbs 14:8)

The simple believe anything, but the prudent give thought to their steps. (Proverbs 14:15)

Desire without knowledge is not good—how much more will hasty feet miss the way! (Proverbs 19:2)

A person's wisdom yields patience; it is to one's glory to overlook an offense. (Proverbs 19:11)

The prudent see danger and take refuge, but the simple keep going and pay the penalty. (Proverbs 22:3)

Devotional

The book of Proverbs often contrasts two types of people: those who are fools (or simple) and those who are wise (or prudent).

Fools are naive and easily influenced. They don't want to do the hard work of thinking things through and asking hard questions. They make assumptions rather than checking the facts. Their decisions are often rushed, impulsive, and focused on short-term, quick-fix solutions.

In contrast, the wise think ahead and exercise good judgment. They are not swept up by impulse or emotion. Prudent people are cautious and carefully consider all relevant factors, possibilities, difficulties, and outcomes. Perhaps most importantly, those who are wise refuse to make quick judgments. They clarify expectations and don't make hasty or unrealistic assumptions of others.

Question to Consider

In what kind of situations is it most difficult for you to pause and give thought to your ways?

Prayer

Lord, grant me a discerning heart so that I might readily distinguish wisdom from foolishness. I ask for grace to resist jumping to conclusions and hastily making assumptions about

others. Help me to patiently consider my actions and my words.
In Jesus' name, amen.

Conclude with Silence (2 minutes)

DAY 2 MORNING/MIDDAY OFFICE

Silence and Stillness before God (2 minutes)

Scripture Reading: Mark 1:35–39

Very early in the morning, while it was still dark, Jesus got
up, left the house and went off to a solitary place, where he
prayed. Simon and his companions went to look for him,
and when they found him, they exclaimed: "Everyone is
looking for you!"

Jesus replied, "Let us go somewhere else—to the nearby
villages—so I can preach there also. That is why I have
come." So he traveled throughout Galilee, preaching in
their synagogues and driving out demons.

Devotional

After a full day of healing, driving out demons, teaching with
authority, and serving the people of Capernaum, Jesus goes off
to a "solitary place" to be still and silent in the presence of God.
As a result, he is able to do the right thing, at the right time, and
with the right heart. He resists the pressure of other people's
expectations and leaves for another city.

For us, this same choice—to turn away from internal and external noise in order to be with God—is work, difficult work. Externally, we face the unrelenting pressure of our culture. Internally, our minds are in constant and frenzied motion. Yet as we learn to live from a wellspring of silence and stillness, we begin to experience an unimaginable richness. In her book *Silence: A User's Guide*, author Maggie Ross explores the many benefits of silence. Here is my summary of just a few:

- We shift away from the artificiality of the surrounding culture toward the beauty of beholding God.
- We grow in our ability to wait and see what unfolds, more trusting of the love of God.
- We realize how foolish our ideas are of how the world works or should work, letting go more easily of judgments, anger, and greed.
- We become more compassionate.
- We influence others for good out of the changes God is doing in and through us.[21]

The effect of practicing silence and stillness with the Father can be dramatic over time, transforming us spiritually, emotionally, and even physically, in ways we cannot anticipate.

Question to Consider

Today, how might you accept the Father's invitation to be silent, "to go off to a solitary place" as Jesus did?

Prayer

> *Lord, help me to remember that you are on the throne, not me.*
> *Help me to trust you with the many things on my to-do list*
> *that I cannot finish. Deliver me from the whirlwind around*
> *me and in me so that the peace and wisdom that emerge out*
> *of stillness and silence might fill me and overflow in love to*
> *others. In Jesus' name, amen.*

Conclude with Silence (2 minutes)

DAY 2 MIDDAY/EVENING OFFICE

Silence and Stillness before God (2 minutes)

Scripture Reading: Acts 5:1–11

Now a man named Ananias, together with his wife
Sapphira, also sold a piece of property. With his wife's full
knowledge he kept back part of the money for himself, but
brought the rest and put it at the apostles' feet.

Then Peter said, "Ananias, how is it that Satan has so
filled your heart that you have lied to the Holy Spirit and
have kept for yourself some of the money you received for the
land? ... You have not lied just to human beings but to God."

When Ananias heard this, he fell down and died. ...

About three hours later his wife came in, not knowing
what had happened. Peter asked her, "Tell me, is this the
price you and Ananias got for the land?"

"Yes," she said, "that is the price."

Peter said to her, "How could you conspire to test the Spirit of the Lord?" . . .

At that moment she fell down at his feet and died. . . . Great fear seized the whole church and all who heard about these events.

Devotional

Lying and pretense are so deeply ingrained in our culture that we rarely notice them. Every culture and family has their own unique way of spinning half-truths, withholding facts, and avoiding awkward moments. We lie with our words, our smiles, our bodies, even our silence. Such deception—of the Holy Spirit, others, and even ourselves—makes it impossible to genuinely love others. Why? Because God is ultimate truth, we unwittingly exclude him whenever we fail to live in truth.

God calls us to walk in truth and follow Jesus who is *the* truth. In fact, the degree to which we live in the truth is the degree to which we are free to have authentic relationships that reflect heaven itself. Our walk with God comes alive and false layers fall off us as our "true self" in Christ within us is awakened.

Only when we end the pretense of superficiality and "niceness" that characterizes so much of Christian culture today will we experience genuine community. With nothing to hide, our stress levels and anxieties decrease and our self-esteem takes deeper root. Why? Because our integrity isn't broken. Peace with God, with others, and with oneself can now permeate our lives.[22]

Question to Consider

Think back over the past few days. In what subtle or not-so-subtle ways did you bend the truth to make yourself look better or avoid someone's disapproval? How was your integrity compromised as a result?

Prayer

> *Lord, grant me courage to look honestly at the areas of my life where I am not living in truth. Help me to recognize when I am saying yes when I prefer to say no, or when I am saying no when I prefer to say yes. Jesus, you are the truth. May I too have the courage to embrace truth in every circumstance and relationship today. Thank you for the safety net of your love. In Jesus' name, amen.*

Conclude with Silence (2 minutes)

DAY 3 MORNING/MIDDAY OFFICE

Silence and Stillness before God (2 minutes)

Scripture Reading: Isaiah 30:15–16, 18

> This is what the Sovereign LORD, the Holy One of
>   Israel, says:
> "In repentance and rest is your salvation,
>   In quietness and trust is your strength,
>   but you would have none of it.

You said, 'No, we will flee on horses.'
    Therefore you will flee!
You said, 'We will ride off on swift horses.'
    Therefore your pursuers will be swift! . . .
Yet the LORD longs to be gracious to you;
    therefore he will rise up to show you compassion.
For the LORD is a God of justice.
    Blessed are all who wait for him!"

Devotional

God offered this promise—to be gracious to his people, Israel—
when they found themselves threatened with the invasion of
Assyria's conquering army, an army that had already overwhelmed the nations around them. Instead of trusting in God
for salvation and strength to face the Assyrians, the Israelites
became impatient and relied on their horses and chariots (the
glamour weapons of that day). They chose short-term relief and
a quick fix. As a result, they fled, making a series of bad decisions
with destructive, long-term consequences.

It's a temptation we too often succumb to today when we
are fearful. Instead of waiting for God to act, we take matters
into our own hands. We make decisions without consulting
God (or others), and we make assumptions about him without
checking them out. Yet God invites us to wait for him and
to rest in his love, allowing him to guide us in our decisions
each day.

Question to Consider

What first comes to mind in response to these words from God for you today: "In repentance and rest is your salvation, in quietness and trust is your strength"?

Prayer

> *Lord, it is so easy for me to take matters into my own hands, especially when faced with trials and pressures. I want to be quiet and trust in you. Show me what it means to wait on you when things appear to be going badly. I want your will, not mine, to be done in my life. In Jesus' name, amen.*

Conclude with Silence (2 minutes)

DAY 3 MIDDAY/EVENING OFFICE

Silence and Stillness before God (2 minutes)

Scripture Reading: Acts 10:9, 11–15, 19–20, 28

> About noon the following day as they were on their journey and approaching the city, Peter went up on the roof to pray. . . . He saw heaven opened and something like a large sheet being let down to earth by its four corners. It contained all kinds of four-footed animals, as well as reptiles and birds. Then a voice told him, "Get up, Peter. Kill and eat."

"Surely not, Lord!" Peter replied. "I have never eaten anything impure or unclean."

The voice spoke to him a second time, "Do not call anything impure that God has made clean." . . .

While Peter was still thinking about the vision, the Spirit said to him, "Simon, three men are looking for you. So get up and go downstairs. Do not hesitate to go with them, for I have sent them." . . .

[Peter] said to them: "You are well aware that it is against our law for a Jew to associate with or visit a Gentile. But God has shown me that I should not call anyone impure or unclean."

Devotional

We are guilty of faulty thinking when we believe something to be true that is false—whether about God, others, or ourselves. Sooner or later, faulty thinking leads to feelings of powerlessness and a great deal of unnecessary pain. Moreover, it results in broken relationships. Three common (and deadly) forms of faulty thinking include:

- *It's all or nothing.* This kind of thinking makes things bigger or more black-and-white than they are.
- *I'm offended.* This refers to taking offense before having all the facts.
- *Things will never change.* The future is fixed and so change is impossible.[23]

The apostle Peter believed things would never change. As a Jew, he had never entered the home of a Gentile. He thought that Jews and Gentiles should forever remain separate, even as the first-century church began to grow. Yet God showed Peter his thinking was wrong, correcting his faulty assumptions and freeing both Peter and those around him for a powerful outpouring of the Holy Spirit in their midst.

Question to Consider

To which of the three forms of faulty thinking are you most susceptible? How has it resulted in unnecessary pain or broken relationships in your life?

Prayer

> *Father, show me where I am engaging in faulty thinking, or making assumptions about a situation or person that are not true. Fill me with the Holy Spirit that I might not be easily misled. Instead, grant me patience and gentleness when I am susceptible to faulty thinking. Help me to mature and see only what is true. In Jesus' name, amen.*

Conclude with Silence (2 minutes)

DAY 4 MORNING/MIDDAY OFFICE

Silence and Stillness before God (2 minutes)

Scripture Reading: Genesis 28:10–17

Jacob left Beersheba and set out for Haran. . . . Taking one of the stones there, he put it under his head and lay down to sleep. He had a dream in which he saw a stairway resting on the earth, with its top reaching to heaven, and the angels of God were ascending and descending on it. There above it stood the LORD, and he said: "I am the LORD, the God of your father Abraham and the God of Isaac. I will give you and your descendants the land on which you are lying. Your descendants will be like the dust of the earth, and you will spread out to the west and to the east, to the north and to the south. All peoples on earth will be blessed through you and your offspring. I am with you and will watch over you wherever you go, and I will bring you back to this land. I will not leave you until I have done what I have promised you."

When Jacob awoke from his sleep, he thought, "Surely the LORD is in this place, and I was not aware of it." He was afraid and said, "How awesome is this place! This is none other than the house of God; this is the gate of heaven."

Devotional

Jacob is running for his life from the rage of his brother Esau. He has manipulated Esau out of the birthright blessing and fled, hoping that a few days away will lessen his brother's hatred. That night, Jacob goes to sleep in an ordinary place and has an extraordinary experience of God. He meets God in a dream, seeing angels ascend back and forth from heaven to earth. Jacob awakens, exclaiming: "Surely the LORD is in this place, and I was not aware of it" (Genesis 28:16).

As poet Elizabeth Barrett Browning has written, "Earth's crammed with heaven." Thomas Merton also says it well:

> Every moment of every event of every man's life on earth plants something in his soul. For just as the wind carries thousands of winged seeds, so each moment brings with it germs of spiritual vitality that come to rest imperceptibly in the minds and hearts of men. Most of these unnumbered seeds perish and are lost because men are not prepared to receive them.[24]

God invites us to that same awareness, to wake and see that he is active in every part of our lives—including our failures, disappointments, betrayals, misunderstandings, shattered dreams, marriage or singleness, anger, and anxieties. We live in a God-soaked world; his love letters to us are everywhere. But too often our spiritual eyes are clouded by fears and stresses. And so we miss him.

Question to Consider

What seeds from God might be coming to rest in your mind and heart today, particularly through a relationship difficulty which you are experiencing?

Prayer

ST. PATRICK'S BREASTPLATE

Christ with me,
Christ before me,
Christ behind me,
Christ in me,
Christ beneath me,
Christ above me,
Christ on my right,
Christ on my left,
Christ when I lie down,
Christ when I sit down,
Christ when I arise,
Christ in the heart of every man who thinks of me,
Christ in the mouth of everyone who speaks of me,
Christ in every eye that sees me,
Christ in every ear that hears me.

I arise today
Through a mighty strength, the invocation of the Trinity,
Through belief in the Threeness,
Through confession of the Oneness of the Creator of creation.

Conclude with Silence (2 minutes)

DAY 4 MIDDAY/EVENING OFFICE

Silence and Stillness before God (2 minutes)

Scripture Reading: James 3:5–10

> The tongue is a small part of the body, but it makes great boasts. Consider what a great forest is set on fire by a small spark. The tongue also is a fire, a world of evil among the parts of the body. It corrupts the whole body, sets the whole course of one's life on fire, and is itself set on fire by hell.
>
> All kinds of animals, birds, reptiles and sea creatures are being tamed and have been tamed by mankind, but no human being can tame the tongue. It is a restless evil, full of deadly poison.
>
> With the tongue we praise our Lord and Father, and with it we curse human beings, who have been made in God's likeness. Out of the same mouth come praise and cursing. My brothers and sisters, this should not be.

Devotional

The ninth commandment reads: "You shall not give false testimony against your neighbor" (Exodus 20:16).

Every time I make an assumption about someone without confirming it, I am at risk for believing a lie about this person. My assumption is just a breath away from misrepresenting reality. Because I have not checked out my assumption with the other person, it is very possible I am believing something untrue and effectively bearing false witness against my neighbor. I am especially prone to this temptation when the other person has hurt or disappointed me. That also makes it more likely I will pass on my false assumption to others.

When we exchange reality for a mental creation (a hidden assumption), we enter a counterfeit world. At that point, we exclude God from our lives because God does not exist outside of reality and truth. We also wreck relationships by creating needless confusion and conflict.[25]

Question to Consider

In what relationship are you making an assumption that may not be true? What small step can you take today to clarify the truth with that person?

Prayer

Lord, I agree that my tongue has the power to do good or evil in people's lives. Forgive me for allowing my words to damage people. Touch my lips and purify my heart. I want the words I speak to impart life to those I interact with today. In Jesus' name, amen.

Conclude with Silence (2 minutes)

DAY 5 MORNING/MIDDAY OFFICE

Silence and Stillness before God (2 minutes)

Scripture Reading: 2 Samuel 7:1–5, 12–13, 18

> After the king was settled in his palace and the LORD had given him rest from all his enemies around him, he said to Nathan the prophet, "Here I am, living in a house of cedar, while the ark of God remains in a tent."
>
> Nathan replied to the king, "Whatever you have in mind, go ahead and do it, for the LORD is with you."
>
> But that night the word of the LORD came to Nathan, saying:
>
> "Go and tell my servant David, 'This is what the LORD says: Are you the one to build me a house to dwell in? . . . When your days are over and you rest with your ancestors, I will raise up your offspring to succeed you, your own flesh and blood, and I will establish his kingdom. He is the one who will build a house for my Name, and I will establish the throne of his kingdom forever. . . .
>
> Then King David went in and sat before the LORD.

Devotional

Many of us have expectations of God that are not met. King David did as well.

Everything had been going right for David. He had consolidated his power. The country was united, and Jerusalem was established as the capital. David was riding a wave of popularity and writing beautiful psalms. He wanted to do something great for God and build him a magnificent temple. The plan looked promising.

God, however, said, no.

David's response—his willingness to immediately set aside his plans and sit in God's presence—offers a model for us when our expectations of God are dashed.

Author and pastor Eugene Peterson writes:

> David *sat*. This may be the most single most critical act that David ever did, the action that put him out of action—more critical than killing Goliath....
>
> David sat. An incredible feat when we begin to understand the conditions under which he did it—so full of desire for God he was, so bursting with plans for God. Stopping David in that condition was like reining in a team of runaway horses. But Nathan stopped him. More accurately, David let himself be stopped by God.[26]

In the same way, something breaks deep within us when we allow ourselves to be stopped by God. It might be our desire to be in control, to manipulate people and circumstances in our favor, or to exert our self-will. Like David, when we allow ourselves to be stopped by God, we slowly learn that we can let go of those things and trust him.

Question to Consider

Identify one situation in your life in which God appears to be saying no or is failing to meet your expectations. How does your response compare to David's?

Prayer

THE WELCOMING PRAYER
Mary Mrozowski

Welcome, welcome, welcome.
I welcome everything that comes to me in this moment
because I know it is for my healing.
I welcome all thoughts, feelings, emotions,
persons, situations and conditions.

I let go of my desire for security.
I let go of my desire for approval.
I let go of my desire for control.

I let go of my desire to change any
situation, condition,
person, or myself.

I open to the
love and presence of God
and
the healing action and grace within.

Conclude with Silence (2 minutes)

DAY 5 MIDDAY/EVENING OFFICE

Silence and Stillness before God (2 minutes)

Scripture Reading: Exodus 32:1–4, 21–24

When the people saw that Moses was so long in coming down from the mountain, they gathered around Aaron and said, "Come, make us gods who will go before us. As for this fellow Moses . . . we don't know what has happened to him."

Aaron answered them, "Take off [your] gold. . . ." He took what they handed him and made it into an idol, cast in the shape of a calf. . . .

[Moses] said to Aaron, "What did these people do to you, that you led them into such great sin?"

"Do not be angry, my lord," Aaron answered. "You know how prone these people are to evil. They said to me, 'Make us gods who will go before us. As for this fellow Moses . . . we don't know what has happened to him.' So I told them, 'Whoever has any gold jewelry, take it off.' Then they gave me the gold, and I threw it into the fire, and out came this calf!"

Devotional

The Israelites are frustrated by Moses' absence as he spends forty days and nights on the mountain with God. So they pressure Aaron to build them an idol they can see. He gives in and builds them an idol in the shape of a golden calf. When Moses returns and confronts him, however, he refuses to take responsibility. Instead, Aaron explains it away, as if the people alone are to blame for the sin of the golden calf.

In the same way, when things don't go our way, our initial reaction is often to deflect responsibility. We might blame our parents, spouses, children, the government, bosses, or coworkers. We might even blame demonic powers or God himself when things are really bad.

Blaming may comfort us, at least for a while, with the illusion that we are in control. However, it actually accomplishes the opposite, stripping us of our God-given personal power and keeping us stuck in immaturity. We mistakenly believe we don't have choices.

As human beings created in Gods' image, we were born with certain rights and responsibilities that enable us to walk in our God-given personal freedom. God gives us freedom to make choices, set boundaries, think for ourselves, and feel. However, we have to take responsibility for what we have been given. We realize we can't change other people, but we can change ourselves in and through the grace of God.[27]

Question to Consider

Who are you tempted to blame for an unhappy or difficult situation in your life? How might you use your God-given freedom to take greater responsibility for one of your choices today?

Prayer

Lord, forgive me for turning away from you by blaming others.
Help me to reclaim the personal freedom you have given me
to make choices. And grant that I may rest in the river of your
love by taking a healthy responsibility for my life. In Jesus'
name, amen.

Conclude with Silence (2 minutes)

Genogram
Your Family

God created us in such a way that we are shaped and formed in relationships, and the relationships that shape us most profoundly are those in our family of origin. Because of sin and brokenness, some of the formation we experienced growing up was flawed or harmful, such as how your family spoke to one another, engaged in conflict, expressed anger, or dealt with certain emotions. As a result of this malformation, we need to relearn what it means to belong to and be formed by the new family of Jesus.

A genogram is a powerful tool that helps us become aware of how the patterns of sin or brokenness in our family of origin—going back three to four generations—can hinder our spiritual and emotional growth in Christ. This awareness empowers us to put off the "old self" and put on our "new selves" in Christ. We die to old ways and learn new ways of being in the world. It's difficult work and requires courage and power, but the power originates not with us but in communion with Jesus, who anchors us in the Father's love and empowers us with the Holy Spirit.

ADDITIONAL RESOURCES

- *The Emotionally Healthy Relationships Workbook*, Session 3
- *The Emotionally Healthy Relationships DVD*, Session 3

DAY 1 MORNING/MIDDAY OFFICE

Silence and Stillness before God (2 minutes)

Scripture Reading: Isaiah 45:1–3 (NASB)

> Thus says the LORD to Cyrus His anointed,
> Whom I have taken by the right hand,
> To subdue nations before him
> And to loose the loins of kings;
> To open doors before him so that gates will not be shut:
> "I will go before you and make the rough places smooth;
> I will shatter the doors of bronze and cut through their
>   iron bars.
> I will give you the treasures of darkness
> And hidden wealth of secret places,
> So that you may know that it is I,
> The LORD, the God of Israel, who calls you by your name."

Devotional

Did you know that God sometimes gives us "treasures of darkness" and reveals the "hidden wealth of secret places"? It's an intriguing promise, isn't it? And it is perhaps especially true when we choose to enter the dark places of the past. Abraham Lincoln's life offers a beautiful illustration of this.

Lincoln struggled with serious depression from a very young age. In his twenties, neighbors sometimes took him into their homes for a week or two at a time to watch over him lest he take his own life. In his twenties and thirties, he had three breakdowns. As a country lawyer with only one year of formal schooling, Lincoln had a history of defeats in running for public office. When he was eventually elected president, he was considered a country bumpkin and a disgrace. In the early years of his presidency, Lincoln's failures and setbacks were a source of vicious public ridicule.

In his book *Lincoln's Melancholy*, author Joshua Wolf Shenk describes how Lincoln was able to integrate his melancholy and his failures into a larger purpose. Shenk argues that it was, in fact, Lincoln's suffering and weaknesses that later fueled his greatness and propelled his personal transformation. Whatever Lincoln's shadow, it is clear that his willingness to acknowledge and integrate all of himself is what enabled him to serve and lead a nation in great danger of falling apart. As a result, he is considered by many to be America's greatest president.[28]

You and I may not be like Abraham Lincoln or be forced to face his challenges, but we can still follow in his footsteps by choosing to embrace the totality of who we are. We can look for treasures in our past areas of darkness. If we are willing to trust him, God can use even our weaknesses and hardships to reveal himself to us.

Question to Consider

What darkness—setback, failure, disappointment, suffering, mistake—first comes to mind when you think about your past?

How might God want to reveal himself to you as you surrender to him the pain of your past?

Prayer

> *Father, I offer my past to you, placing my trust in the reality that you are the Lord of history, including my history. I cannot see all you see, but I ask you to help me rest in your love and power, trusting that you are working out a good plan in and through me—for my sake and for the sake of the world. In Jesus' name, amen.*

Conclude with Silence (2 minutes)

DAY 1 MIDDAY/EVENING OFFICE

Silence and Stillness before God (2 minutes)

Scripture Reading: Job 42:1–6, 12–13, 16

Then Job replied to the LORD:

> "I know that you can do all things;
>   no purpose of yours can be thwarted.
> You asked, 'Who is this that obscures my plans
>   without knowledge?'
>   Surely I spoke of things I did not understand,
>   things too wonderful for me to know.
> "You said, 'Listen now, and I will speak;

> I will question you,
>   and you shall answer me.'
> My ears had heard of you
>   but now my eyes have seen you.
> Therefore I despise myself
>   and repent in dust and ashes." . . .

The LORD blessed the latter part of Job's life more than the former part. He had fourteen thousand sheep, six thousand camels, a thousand yoke of oxen and a thousand donkeys. And he also had seven sons and three daughters. . . .

After this, Job lived a hundred and forty years; he saw his children and their children to the fourth generation.

Devotional

Job is a man of great faith and character, and one of the godliest, most respected men in his community. Yet he suffers deeply in every way—physically, socially, spiritually, and emotionally. All the forces of evil come against him. Enemies invade. Lightning strikes. A tornado unleashes its fury. The unthinkable happens—one of the world's richest men is suddenly reduced to poverty. Then all ten of his children are killed in a terrible natural disaster. Finally, he becomes so sick he is virtually unrecognizable.

During this dark night of the soul—a season in which God feels absent—Job struggles. He doubts. He questions. He gets angry. He wants to die. But he continues to engage with God, to believe in the goodness of God, even as he tries to make sense of his suffering.

In the end, he is spiritually transformed and brought to a new place by the Lord, who "blessed the latter part of Job's life more than the [first]" (Job 42:12).

The story of Job is meant to encourage us to trust the living God with the many "deaths" we experience in our lives. Why? Because there are many rich fruits that will blossom in our lives as a result of the pain and losses of our past. We can trust Jesus, who shows us that resurrection and transformation *always* follow suffering and death.[29]

Question to Consider

How might God be transforming you through the pain and losses of your past?

Prayer

> *Lord Jesus, when I think about the losses of my past, I admit I don't understand why you allowed such pain. Looking at Job helps, but I still struggle to believe that something good might come from it. Grant me the courage to feel, to pay attention, and to wait on you. May the prayer of Job be mine: "My ears had heard of you but now my eyes have seen you." In Jesus' name, amen.*

Conclude with Silence (2 minutes)

DAY 2 MORNING/MIDDAY OFFICE

Silence and Stillness before God (2 minutes)

Scripture Reading: 2 Corinthians 12:7–10

In order to keep me from becoming conceited, I was given a thorn in my flesh, a messenger of Satan, to torment me. Three times I pleaded with the Lord to take it away from me. But he said to me, "My grace is sufficient for you, for my power is made perfect in weakness." Therefore I will boast all the more gladly about my weaknesses, so that Christ's power may rest on me. That is why, for Christ's sake, I delight in weaknesses, in insults, in hardships, in persecutions, in difficulties. For when I am weak, then I am strong.

Devotional

The painful disappointments in our past and the hardships we face in the present are often the last places we look for God. They appear to hold us back and limit our future. However, if we fail to look for God *in* these limits and sufferings, we often bypass him.

When we look for God in our limitations—instead of putting all our energy into trying to eliminate or get around them—we begin to see that our very limitations have the potential to become our greatest source of strength. Remember the words of the apostle Paul? God's power is made perfect in our *weaknesses*, not in our strengths (2 Corinthians 12:9).

Consider these examples from Scripture:

- Moses was limited by the fact that he was slow of speech and his past was filled with failure. God makes it clear that he is present in and through Moses' limitations: "Who gave human beings their mouths? . . . Is it not I, the LORD? Now go; I will help you speak and will teach you what to say" (Exodus 4:11–12). Moses then leads two to three million people for the next forty years in the power of God.

- The prophet Jeremiah was limited by a melancholy disposition and repeated rejection. He cursed the day he was born and wanted to die (Jeremiah 20:14–18). Yet God was present in and through the limits of his temperament and life situation, giving him insights about the heart of God that still touch and teach God's people today.

- Abraham was limited by Sarah's barrenness and decades of wondering if he would ever have a rightful heir. He suffered under that reality, yet he met God in extraordinary ways through his journey of faith. When ninety-year-old Sarah became pregnant with Isaac, God fulfilled his promise to make Abraham the father of many nations, including all of us (Genesis 17:4, Romans 4:17). Abraham's story provides us revelations of who God is—all of which came out of Abraham's hardships and limits.

The limits and wounds we carry are often the arena in which God demonstrates his power and gives us his gifts in disguise. It is one of the most counterintuitive and difficult truths in Scripture to embrace because it flies in the face of our natural tendency to want to be in control and run the world.[30] And yet, it is precisely in these difficult places that God longs to teach us, provide for us, and reveal himself to us.

Question to Consider

How might a present limit or past failure be God's gift of love for you, and a gift you can give to the world?

Prayer

Lord, you know I resist limits and looking at painful disappointments. They are the last place I want to look for you. Help me to see how the painful parts of my past or present might be opportunities for me to see you clearly and discern how you might want to use me in the future. In Jesus' name, amen.

Conclude with Silence (2 minutes)

DAY 2 MIDDAY/EVENING OFFICE

Silence and Stillness before God (2 minutes)

Scripture Reading: Mark 15:33–39

At noon, darkness came over the whole land until three in the afternoon. And at three in the afternoon Jesus cried out in a loud voice, *"Eloi, Eloi, lema sabachthani?"* (which means, "My God, my God, why have you forsaken me?").

When some of those standing near heard this, they said, "Listen, he's calling Elijah."

Someone ran, filled a sponge with wine vinegar, put it on a staff, and offered it to Jesus to drink. "Now leave him alone. Let's see if Elijah comes to take him down," he said.

With a loud cry, Jesus breathed his last.

The curtain of the temple was torn in two from top to bottom. And when the centurion, who stood there in front of Jesus, saw how he died, he said, "Surely this man was the Son of God!"

Devotional

When we courageously face the wounds and failures of our past and our family of origin, it can fill us with fear or dread. "Where was God?" we wonder. "Why did he allow these things to happen?" It can be a painful and confusing experience.

When Jesus cried out to God on the cross, the Father did not answer. Yet, God was powerfully present in the silence. Jesus remained with his Father even though he didn't "feel him"—and in the process, he teaches us what true faith is.

True faith allows us to call on God even when we do not feel his presence. On the spiritual journey, we can become so dependent on feelings that when we don't "feel God" in the way we think we should, we give up or take matters into our own hands. *But growing up spiritually requires moving past loving our feelings about God to loving God for who he is*—even when he seems silent and distant. For this reason, Scripture teaches us that God's silence, very often, is actually a gift and an expression of his love for us. In fact, we discover that when God seems most absent, he is closer to us and more powerfully at work than ever.

Question to Consider

How might you hold on to God when he is silent and you don't "feel his presence"?

Prayer

> *Father, it is easy for me to let my feelings or my circumstances be the indicator of whether you are present or absent in my life. Help me to see that even though I may not feel you in the ways I would like, you are still working powerfully in my life. In Jesus' name, amen.*

Conclude with Silence (2 minutes)

DAY 3 MORNING/MIDDAY OFFICE

Silence and Stillness before God (2 minutes)

Scripture Reading: Genesis 12:1–4

> The LORD had said to Abram, "Go from your country, your people and your father's household to the land I will show you.

"I will make you into a great nation,
     and I will bless you.
I will make your name great,
     and you will be a blessing.
I will bless those who bless you,
     and whoever curses you I will curse;
and all peoples on earth
     will be blessed through you."

So Abram went, as the LORD had told him; and Lot went with him. Abram was seventy-five years old when he set out from Harran.

Devotional

When the Bible uses the word *family*, it refers not just to parents and children but to an entire extended family over three to four generations. That means your family, in the biblical sense, includes your brothers, sisters, uncles, aunts, grandparents, great-grandparents, great-uncles and aunts, and significant others going back to the mid-1800s. The blessings and sins of this extended family over generations profoundly impact who we are today. For this reason, we say, "Jesus may be in your heart, but Grandpa is in your bones," meaning the proverbial grandpas cast a long shadow over the generations in any family.

In order to respond to God's invitation and receive God's promise, Abraham had to leave his family behind. Much as we have to do today, he had to put off the sinful and unhealthy patterns of his family of origin and learn to do life God's way in God's family.

Kaethe Weingarten, a professor at Harvard Medical School, has done extensive research on how the traumatic experiences of one generation are passed to those in the next generation. She studied, for example, Holocaust survivors and their families, survivors of terrorist attacks, and children of parents with post-traumatic stress disorder (PTSD). She writes:

> What is passed is not the trauma itself, but its impact.... Silence is a key mechanism by which trauma in one generation is communicated to the next. We are accustomed to think of silence as an absence of sound, but it functions in families in much more complex and confusing ways. Silence can communicate a wealth of meanings. It is its own map: Don't go there; don't say that; don't touch; too much; too little; this hurts; this doesn't.... Silence ... co-occurs with numbers of other phenomena. Shame, a painful affect in which one feels exposed as "fundamentally deficient in some vital way as a human being" is one of them.[31]

Scripture teaches us that we can unlearn negative patterns that were passed on to us over generations. And by God's grace and power, we can learn healthier ways to do life in the new family of Jesus. Change and freedom are possible through the truth that sets us free.

Question to Consider

What first comes to mind when you think about an unhealthy message that was communicated by silence in your family of origin? How do you sense Jesus may be inviting you to unlearn that message in order to live in a healthier way in God's family?

Prayer

PRAYER OF ABANDONMENT

Charles de Foucauld

My Father,
I abandon myself to you.
Make of me what you will.

Whatever you make of me,
I thank you.
I am ready for everything.
I accept everything.

Provided that your will be done in me,
In all your creatures,
I desire nothing else, Lord.

I put my soul in your hands,
I give it to you, Lord,
With all the love in my heart,
Because I love you,

And because it is for me a need of love
To give myself,
To put myself in your hands unreservedly,
With infinite trust.
For you are my Father.[32]

Conclude with Silence (2 minutes)

DAY 3 MIDDAY/EVENING OFFICE

Silence and Stillness before God (2 minutes)

Scripture Reading: Luke 2:41–43, 49–52

Every year Jesus' parents went to Jerusalem for the Festival of the Passover.

When he was twelve years old, they went up to the festival, according to the custom. After the festival was over, while his parents were returning home, the boy Jesus stayed behind in Jerusalem, but they were unaware of it....

"Why were you searching for me?" he asked. "Didn't you know I had to be in my Father's house?" But they did not understand what he was saying to them.

Then he went down to Nazareth with them and was obedient to them. But his mother treasured all these things in her heart. And Jesus grew in wisdom and stature, and in favor with God and man.

Devotional

Jesus spent nearly thirty years with a seemingly delayed destiny before he began his public ministry. We learn about him at age twelve in this passage, but then hear little else until he is begins his ministry as an adult. We know only that he "grew in wisdom and in stature and in favor with God and all the people" (Luke 2:52 NLT), embracing the hidden, slow work of God in him during those unseen years.

Author Alicia Britt Chole writes compellingly about these anonymous years in Jesus' life:

Only three years, less than 10 percent, of Jesus' days are visible through the writings of the Bible. Over 90 percent of his earthly life is submerged in the unseen.... Onlookers saw only the tip of the iceberg of who Jesus truly was, and they could have never imagined the indestructible greatness growing just beneath the surface of Jesus' unapplauded life....

"What would Jesus do?" we ask sincerely.... Well, for starters, he embraced a life of hiddenness.... With his life (and with ours), it is critical that we not mistake *unseen* for *unimportant*.... From God's perspective, anonymous seasons are sacred spaces. They are quite literally formative; to be rested in, not rushed through— and most definitely never to be regretted.... Hidden years are the surprising birthplace of true spiritual greatness."[33]

The pattern of Jesus' life is meant to be a model for us. We too are to make disciples, carry our cross, and access resurrection power. Our anonymous, unseen seasons are sacred and not to be rushed. Just as he did in Jesus, God is birthing true spiritual greatness in us during our times and places of hiddenness.

Question to Consider

How might God be doing an important but unseen work in, through, and in spite of any hiddenness you are experiencing right now?

Prayer

> *Father, sometimes I act as though I am in charge of running the world. Forgive me. Teach me to be patient and to remain hidden when appropriate. May I not rush your slow, sacred work of forming Christ in me—even when I don't understand what you are doing. In Jesus' name, amen.*

Conclude with Silence (2 minutes)

DAY 4 MORNING/MIDDAY OFFICE

Silence and Stillness before God (2 minutes)

Scripture Reading: Luke 4:1–12

> Jesus, full of the Holy Spirit, left the Jordan and was led by the Spirit into the wilderness, where for forty days he was

tempted by the devil. He ate nothing during those days, and at the end of them he was hungry.

The devil said to him, "If you are the Son of God, tell this stone to become bread."

Jesus answered, "It is written: '[Humans] shall not live on bread alone.'"

The devil led him up to a high place and showed him in an instant all the kingdoms of the world. And he said to him, "I will give you all their authority and splendor; it has been given to me, and I can give it to anyone I want to. If you worship me, it will all be yours."

Jesus answered, "It is written: 'Worship the Lord your God and serve him only.'"

The devil led him to Jerusalem and had him stand on the highest point of the temple. "If you are the Son of God," he said, "throw yourself down from here. For it is written:

"'He will command his angels concerning you
     to guard you carefully;
they will lift you up in their hands,
     so that you will not strike your foot against
     a stone.'"

Jesus answered, "It is said: 'Do not put the Lord your God to the test.'"

Devotional

Life is filled with desert experiences, times when we find ourselves in seemingly barren places and susceptible to temptation by the Evil One. These experiences are painful, difficult, and disorienting. This is perhaps nowhere more evident than when we look closely at our family histories and explore their impact on us. We suddenly find ourselves in a desert, wondering how to integrate difficult past experiences into a hopeful future.

Yet Jesus models for us the importance of allowing the Holy Spirit to lead us into and through these places so God can do a profound work in us. Every spiritual journey takes us into the hardest realities of our lives. We are invited by God to surrender to this process and meet the darkness we harbor within. If we refuse to do so, we will inevitably project that darkness outward, making others our enemies. Desert experiences can do a profound work in us—but only with our consent. Note that Jesus goes into the desert "full of the Holy Spirit" (Luke 4:1), and then emerges from the desert "in the power of the Spirit" (Luke 4:14). The desert has deepened and empowered him, making him ready to begin his active ministry.

God uses hard times, sufferings, and trials to produce maturity and greatness in us (James 1:2–4). The key is that we patiently remain with Jesus, trusting God to reveal over the course of our lives a delicate and beautiful pattern visible only in hindsight.

Question to Consider

What is one specific area in your life that God is inviting you to patiently trust him today?

Prayer

> *Lord, give me the courage to follow you on the unique journey you have for me, even when it leads me into a desert. Help me surrender my need and desire to be in control of people and circumstances. Grant me the power today to simply rest in your arms of love. In Jesus' name, amen.*

Conclude with Silence (2 minutes)

DAY 4 MIDDAY/EVENING OFFICE

Silence and Stillness before God (2 minutes)

Scripture Reading: Genesis 37:17b–20; 50:19–21

So Joseph went after his brothers and found them near Dothan. But they saw him in the distance, and before he reached them, they plotted to kill him.

"Here comes that dreamer!" they said to each other. "Come now, let's kill him and throw him into one of these cisterns and say that a ferocious animal devoured him. Then we'll see what comes of his dreams." . . .

But Joseph said to them, "Don't be afraid. Am I in the place of God? You intended to harm me, but God intended it for good to accomplish what is now being done, the saving of many lives. So then, don't be afraid. I will provide for you and your children." And he reassured them and spoke kindly to them.

Devotional

One of the great wonders of the sovereignty or the "bigness" of God is the way he moves invisibly in and through human affairs. We observe this powerfully in Joseph's life as he suffers a number of traumatic experiences at the hands of his family and ends up living exiled in Egypt for decades. Even when suffering from one setback after another, Joseph trusts that God is somehow leading him into a larger purpose. Scholar Walter Brueggemann writes:

> The theme of the Joseph narrative concerns God's hidden and decisive power which works in and through but also against human forms of power.... The theme is that God is working out his purpose through and in spite of Egypt, through and in spite of Joseph and his brothers.... The evil plans of human folks do not defeat God's purpose. Instead, they unwittingly become ways in which God's plan is furthered.[34]

Phillips Brooks, a seventeenth-century American preacher, summarized God's redemptive work this way:

> You must let God teach you the only way to get rid of your past is to make a future out of it. God will waste nothing.[35]

God never discards any of our past when we surrender ourselves to him. He is the Lord God Almighty! He fashions every mistake, sin, and detour we take in the journey of life into a future of blessings. Much of how God accomplishes this remains a mystery. We are simply invited to trust his goodness and love.

Question to Consider

What hopes and dreams come to mind when you consider that God wastes nothing?

Prayer

Father, I trust in your goodness and love today. You placed me in my particular family in a particular place and moment in human history. All that I have, I have received from you (1 Corinthians 4:7). While I cannot see all you see, I rest in your love and trust in your power today. In Jesus' name, amen.

Conclude with Silence (2 minutes)

DAY 5 MORNING/MIDDAY OFFICE

Silence and Stillness before God (2 minutes)

Scripture Reading: Isaiah 55:6–9

> Seek the LORD while he may be found;
> > call on him while he is near.
> Let the wicked forsake their ways
> > and the unrighteous their thoughts.
> Let them turn to the LORD, and he will have mercy
> > on them,

and to our God, for he will freely pardon.
"For my thoughts are not your thoughts,
    neither are your ways my ways,"
    declares the LORD.
"As the heavens are higher than the earth,
    so are my ways higher than your ways
    and my thoughts than your thoughts."

Devotional

When we are suffering, one of the most powerful tools we have available to us is the ability to find meaning and embrace hope in the midst of it. This was both the insight and lived experience of Viktor Frankl, a psychiatrist and survivor of four Nazi concentration camps. Only one in twenty-eight people who entered the camps emerged alive. Frankl witnessed that those who knew there was a task waiting for them to fulfill were most likely to survive:

> The prisoner who lost hope in the future—his future—was doomed. With his loss of belief in the future, he also lost his spiritual hold; he let himself decline and became subject to mental and physical decay. . . .
>
> Whenever there was an opportunity for it, one had to give them a why—an aim—for their lives, in order to strengthen them to bear the terrible *how* of their existence. Woe to him who had no more sense in his life, no aim, no purpose, and therefore no point in carrying on. He was soon lost. . . .

It did not really matter what we expected from life,
but rather what life expected from us. . . . Life ultimately
means . . . to fulfill the tasks which it constantly sets for
each individual.

A man who becomes conscious of the responsibility he
bears toward a human being who affectionately waits for
him, or to an unfinished work, will never be able to throw
away his life. He knows the "why" for his existence, and will
be able to bear almost any "how." . . .

They form man's destiny, which is different and unique
for each individual. . . . [Thus] man's main concern is not to
gain pleasure or to avoid pain but rather to see a meaning
in his life.[36]

When confronted by great evil and suffering, such as the
Holocaust, it's only natural to ask, *Why?* The answer remains
shrouded in mystery. What we do know, however, is that
God's thoughts are not our thoughts, nor are his ways our
ways. And we know that out of the greatest evil ever done
on earth—the crucifixion of Jesus—has come the greatest
good in history.

So God invites us to trust him, placing our hope in his
goodness, resting assured that he is so great and sovereign he
will ultimately transform all evil into good.

Question to Consider

How is God inviting you to trust him today?

Prayer

*Lord, your ways are so much higher than mine, and your
thoughts are so much larger than mine. While I may not
always see the end from the beginning, I trust you today with
my future. And I offer my life to you for the work that you have
appointed me to do. In Jesus' name, amen.*

Conclude with Silence (2 minutes)

DAY 5 MIDDAY/EVENING OFFICE

Silence and Stillness (2 minutes)

Scripture Reading: Psalm 130:1–2, 5–7

> Out of the depths I cry to you, LORD;
>> Lord, hear my voice.
> Let your ears be attentive
>> to my cry for mercy. . . .
> I wait for the LORD, my whole being waits,
>> and in his word I put my hope.
> I wait for the Lord
>> more than watchmen wait for the morning,
>> more than watchmen wait for the morning.
> Israel, put your hope in the LORD,
>> for with the LORD is unfailing love
>> and with him is full redemption.

Devotional

This psalm captures the reality that "waiting for the Lord" is a foundational principle of the spiritual life. In fact, when we are waiting, we are doing one of our most important spiritual tasks; we are allowing God to work and grow our soul. Here is how author and pastor Eugene Peterson describes the purpose and significance of waiting on God:

> The long and short of it is that there is a lot more going on on the way than getting to a destination. And there is a lot more going on on the way than what we are doing. There is what God is doing. Which is why we "wait on the Lord." We stop, whether by choice or through circumstance, so that we can be alert and attentive and receptive to what God is doing in and for us, in and for others, on the way. We wait for our souls to catch up with our bodies. Waiting for the Lord is a large part of what we do on the way because the largest part of what takes place on the way is what God is doing, what God is saying. . . . The waiting is not just an indolent "waiting around." We wait "for the morning," which is to say we wait in hope. We wait for God to do what we cannot do for ourselves "in the depths." When he has done it, we are once more on the way."[37]

The need for such waiting on the Lord is perhaps nowhere more necessary than when we consider our histories and our family of origin. *Where was God? Why did he allow certain events to occur? Why did he allow me to be born into that particular family at that particular time? And for what purpose?*

God tells us that we see and know only partially, but someday we shall know fully, just as we are fully known (see 1 Corinthians 13:12). In the meantime, he invites us to wait on him, trusting in his wisdom and love that surpasses human knowledge.

Question to Consider

Name one area in your life where you are curious of what God might be doing—especially as it relates to your family of origin history. How might he be inviting you to wait patiently for him?

Prayer

> *Let nothing disturb you.*
> *Let nothing frighten you.*
> *All things pass away.*
> *God is unchangeable.*
> *Patience gains everything.*
> *He who clings to God wants nothing.*
> *God alone is sufficient.*[38]
>
> —Teresa of Avila

Conclude with Silence (2 minutes)

Explore the
Iceberg

DAILY OFFICES
Week Four

To "explore the iceberg" is to look beneath the surface of our lives, identifying the hidden but powerful forces that shape the way we navigate choices and relationships. By acknowledging and naming these realities, we raise our emotional awareness, which in turn enables us to process our emotions in a healthy way, and to integrate them into our discernment of God's will.

In the Psalms, King David offers us a powerful example of this when he pours out his heart to God (see Psalm 62:8). When we embark on a similar journey, we experience a newfound grace to be increasingly approachable, kind, and gentle—not only with God, but also with those around us.

ADDITIONAL RESOURCES

- *The Emotionally Healthy Relationships Workbook*, Session 4
- *The Emotionally Healthy Relationships DVD*, Session 4

DAY 1 MORNING/MIDDAY OFFICE

Silence and Stillness before God (2 minutes)

Scripture Reading: Matthew 26:36–44

Then Jesus went with his disciples to a place called Gethsemane, and he said to them, "Sit here while I go over there and pray." He took Peter and the two sons of Zebedee along with him, and he began to be sorrowful and troubled. Then he said to them, "My soul is overwhelmed with sorrow to the point of death. Stay here and keep watch with me."

Going a little farther, he fell with his face to the ground and prayed, "My Father, if it is possible, may this cup be taken from me. Yet not as I will, but as you will."

Then he returned to his disciples and found them sleeping. "Couldn't you men keep watch with me for one hour?" he asked Peter. "Watch and pray so that you will not fall into temptation. The spirit is willing, but the flesh is weak."

He went away a second time and prayed, "My Father, if it is not possible for this cup to be taken away unless I drink it, may your will be done."

When he came back, he again found them sleeping, because their eyes were heavy. So he left them and went away once more and prayed the third time, saying the same thing.

Devotional

In some Christian circles, repressing or disavowing authentic emotion is considered a virtue or perhaps even a gift of Spirit. Denying anger, ignoring pain, skipping over depression, running from loneliness, and avoiding doubt are not only considered normal but actually virtuous ways of living out one's spiritual life.

But this is not the model we find in Jesus, who freely expressed his emotions without shame or embarrassment:

- He shed tears (Luke 19:41).
- He was filled with joy (Luke 10:21).
- He felt overwhelmed with grief (Mark 14:34).
- He was angry and distressed (Mark 3:5).
- He was sorrowful and troubled (Matthew 26:37).
- His heart was moved with compassion (Luke 7:13).
- He expressed amazement (Mark 6:6, Luke 7:9).

Jesus was anything but an emotionally frozen Messiah.

In Gethsemane, we see a fully human Jesus—anguished, sorrowful, and spiritually overwhelmed. He is pushed to the extremes of his human limits: "and being in anguish, he prayed more earnestly, and his sweat was like drops of blood falling to the ground" (Luke 22:44).

So, we must ask ourselves: Where did we get the idea that acknowledging and expressing authentic emotion is somehow less than spiritual? And why do we believe that we can—or somehow should—grow in *spiritual* maturity without simulta-neously growing in *emotional* maturity?[39]

Question to Consider

In light of Jesus' ability to express his feelings to his closest friends, how would you describe your ability to do the same? Do you do so easily, awkwardly, with great difficulty, or never?

Prayer

> *Lord, help me to slow down enough to feel and acknowledge what is going on inside me. Grant me the courage to enter into honest and authentic relationship—with you, with others, and with myself—trusting that you will carry me. Help me to rest and relax in you as I take the risk to be more transparent and vulnerable with my emotions. In Jesus' name, amen.*

Conclude with Silence (2 minutes)

DAY 1 MIDDAY/EVENING OFFICE

Silence and Stillness God before God (2 minutes)

Scripture Reading: Job 3:1–5a; 6:1–4

After this, Job opened his mouth and cursed the day of his birth. He said:

"May the day of my birth perish,
 and the night that said, 'A boy is conceived!'
That day—may it turn to darkness;
 may God above not care about it;
 may no light shine on it.
May gloom and utter darkness claim it once more. . . .
If only my anguish could be weighed
 and all my misery be placed on the scales!
It would surely outweigh the sand of the seas—
 no wonder my words have been impetuous.
The arrows of the Almighty are in me,
 my spirit drinks in their poison;
 God's terrors are marshaled against me."

Devotional

Job was one of the richest men in the world in his day. In contemporary terms, his assets would have included a fleet of Rolls-Royces, private airplanes, yachts, thriving global companies, and significant real estate holdings. "He was the greatest man among all the people of the East" (Job 1:3). After a series of natural disasters, however, something unthinkable happens— Job is reduced to poverty and his ten children are killed in a terrible natural disaster. When he attempts to get on his feet, he is infected with "sore boils" from the soles of his feet to the top of his head. Physically, it looks like he is about to die at any moment. His wife's compassionate counsel? "Curse God and die" (Job 2:9).

Job finds himself alone, isolated, and living outside the city walls in the garbage dump. As the text indicates, Job is very angry. But there is a lesson for us even in Job's anger. Here is how author Philip Yancey describes it:

> One bold message in the Book of Job is that you can say anything to God. Throw at him your grief, your anger, your doubt, your bitterness, your betrayal, your disappointment—he can absorb them all. As often as not, spiritual giants of the Bible are shown *contending* with God. They prefer to go away limping, like Jacob, rather than to shut God out. In this respect, the Bible prefigures a tenet of modern psychology: you can't really deny your feelings or make them disappear, so you might as well express them. God can deal with every human response save one. He cannot abide the response I fall back on instinctively: an attempt to ignore him or treat him as though he does not exist. That response never once occurred to Job."[40]

In the same way, God invites us to feel our emotions, experiencing them without self-condemnation, and exploring them in his loving presence.

Question to Consider

In what ways do you tend to suppress or deny difficult emotions—anger, sadness, fear—rather than admit them to yourself and God?

Prayer

> *Father, the idea of being emotionally transparent with you—*
> *especially when my emotions are raw—is very difficult. In fact,*
> *it almost seems disrespectful. Thank you, Lord, that you love*
> *all of me—the good, the bad, and the ugly—and that your*
> *love is without conditions. In Jesus' name, amen.*

Conclude with Silence (2 minutes)

DAY 2 MORNING/MIDDAY OFFICE

Silence and Stillness before God (2 minutes)

Scripture Reading: Hebrews 5:7–8

During the days of Jesus' life on earth, he offered up prayers
and petitions with fervent cries and tears to the one who
could save him from death, and he was heard because of
his reverent submission. Son though he was, he learned
obedience from what he suffered.

Devotional

The way we express and respond to certain emotions is directly
related to how these emotions were handled in our family of origin. If your parents or caregivers limited their range of acceptable
emotions, it naturally follows that you would do the same.

Children who are not allowed to express certain feelings
tend to conclude something like this: "If these emotions are

unacceptable, then there is no reason to feel them in the first place." They also begin to pick up on the family's unwritten rules, such as "good people smile a lot," and "a loving person doesn't get angry." When children then carry these unwritten rules into adulthood, they create relational barriers that stifle authenticity and meaningful connection.

Unfortunately, some Christian communities reinforce this crippling approach, perpetuating a culture in which people routinely deal with distressing feelings in muddled and undifferentiated ways. The result is that many Christians feel unspiritual for attempting to sort out or express their feelings.

We tend to emphasize joyfulness, overcoming obstacles, and being strong in Christ. We are told to rejoice even when sad or angry. And we are certainly not to share our fears since the Bible is filled with commands not to fear. We might even consider these emotions to be practically synonymous with sin. We hope that by suppressing and ignoring them, they might somehow disappear. In doing so, we are a long way from the example of Jesus, who offered up "fervent cries and tears to [his Father]" (Hebrews 5:7–8).

This superficial and incomplete understanding of Scripture severely stunts our spiritual growth and our ability to love well. It also erodes any possibility of developing authentic Christian community. We build walls of separation and cannot truly see one another. We fear vulnerability and lie about what is going on inside us. So, instead of inviting people to become more fully alive, we unintentionally create a religious subculture that constricts and deprives people from experiencing the full range of their God-given humanity.[41]

Question to Ponder

Growing up, what messages did you pick up from your family about anger, sadness, and fear? How have those messages impacted you as an adult?

Prayer

Father, I admit that I prefer to ignore my pain and skim over my fears, and that I am often embarrassed to openly share with you what is going on inside me—as if you don't know it all anyway. Transform me, Lord, that I might be vulnerable and honest— with you, with myself, and with others. In Jesus' name, amen.

Conclude with Silence (2 minutes)

DAY 2 MIDDAY/EVENING OFFICE

Silence and Stillness before God (2 minutes)

Scripture Reading: Psalm 32:8–10

I will instruct you and teach you in the way you
   should go;
      I will counsel you with my loving eye on you.
Do not be like the horse or the mule,
   which have no understanding

but must be controlled by bit and bridle
    or they will not come to you.
Many are the woes of the wicked,
    but the LORD's unfailing love
    surrounds the one who trusts in him.

Devotional

When it comes to exploring our emotions, we might wonder something like this: *If I allow myself to feel all my emotions all the time, won't it lead to irrational behavior? Or worse, lead me down wrong roads in my following Jesus? How can I discern God's will and God's leading if my feelings are unreliable?*

The answers to these questions might surprise you.

More than 450 years ago, Ignatius of Loyola, founder of the Jesuits, developed a set of guidelines that respected the important place of our emotions in discerning God's will. He rightly emphasized the foundation of a complete commitment to do God's will, obey Scripture, and seek wise counsel. Yet, in addition, he provided excellent guidelines for sorting out how God speaks to us through our emotions. The issue is not, he argued, to blindly follow our feelings, but to acknowledge them as *part* of the way God communicates to us. Author Thomas Green explains it well:

> It is essential to spiritual discernment that we be in touch with our feelings. How many of us, however, are really so in touch? How many can "name, claim, tame and aim" the

feelings within us which are the raw material of discernment? Many say it is very difficult to know God since we do not see him, hear him, or touch him as we do another human being. That is true, of course, but I have become convinced that the greatest obstacle to real discernment (and to genuine growth in prayer) is not the intangible nature of God, but our own lack of self-knowledge—even our *unwillingness* to know ourselves as we truly are. Almost all of us wear masks, not only when facing others but even when looking in the mirror.[42]

Taking the time, then, to remove those masks so we can feel deeply does not hinder our discernment, but actually positions us to hear God's voice of love that calls out to us through our emotions.

Question to Consider

How might God be inviting you to be still today so that you may be more aware of your feelings and better hear his voice?

Prayer

Father, even though it's hard for me, I invite you to speak to me through my emotions—to lead and guide me by helping me to be in touch with what I am truly feeling. Give me the grace to "name, claim, tame, and aim" my feelings so that I can better discern your will for my life. In Jesus' name, amen.

Conclude with Silence (2 minutes)

DAY 3 MORNING/MIDDAY OFFICE

Silence and Stillness before God (2 minutes)

Scripture Reading: Psalm 22:1-2, 7-8, 12-13

> My God, my God, why have you forsaken me?
>> Why are you so far from saving me,
>> so far from my cries of anguish?
>
> My God, I cry out by day, but you do not answer,
>> by night, but I find no rest. . . .
>
> All who see me mock me;
>> they hurl insults, shaking their heads.
>
> "He trusts in the LORD," they say,
>> "let the LORD rescue him.
>
> Let him deliver him,
>> since he delights in him." . . .
>
> Do not be far from me,
>> for trouble is near
>> and there is no one to help.
>
> Many bulls surround me;
>> strong bulls of Bashan encircle me.
>
> Roaring lions that tear their prey
>> open their mouths wide against me.

Devotional

David, a man after God's own heart, beautifully models the seamless integration of his emotions and his hunger for God.

In the Psalms, we see that he holds nothing back, freely pouring out his fears, despair, anger, and shame. In fact, the wide range of his emotional ups and downs is sometimes shocking to our modern sensibilities. What does David understand about the integration of emotions and faith that we don't?

In *The Cry of the Soul,* authors Dan Allender and Tremper Longman III offer a partial answer:

> Perhaps a better explanation for why it's so difficult to feel our feelings is that *all* emotion, positive or negative, opens the door to the nature of reality. All of us prefer to avoid pain—but even more, we want to escape reality.
>
> Even when life is delightful, joy is fleeting and its brief appearance only opens our desire for more. Pleasure holds a wistful incompleteness because, even at its best, it is a poor picture of what we were meant to enjoy. As a result, we never feel completely satisfied with our present life, no matter how well things go. Anticipation inevitably carries with it disappointment and longing.
>
> Emotion propels us into the tragic recognition that we are not home. . . .
>
> There are times when lack of emotion is simply a byproduct of hardness and arrogance. The Scriptures reveal that this absence of feelings is often a refusal to face the sorrow of life and the hunger for heaven.[43]

David is well known for being a man after God's own heart. What few realize is how closely this was tied to his emotional awareness (his openness about his losses and disappointments) and his passionate heart for God (his longing to see him face-to-face).

Question to Consider

How might your prayer life change if, like David, you could bring to God what is *actually* in you and not what you think *should* be in you?

Prayer

Lord, today I bring you all of my emotions: my anger (list what you are angry about), my sadness (list what you are sad about), and my fear (list what you are afraid of). Help me this day to embrace the full range of my emotions, just as David did. In Jesus' name, amen.

Conclude with Silence (2 minutes)

DAY 3 MIDDAY/EVENING OFFICE

Silence and Stillness before God (2 minutes)

Scripture Reading: Daniel 3:15b–18

"If you are ready to fall down and worship the image I made, very good. But if you do not worship it, you will be thrown immediately into a blazing furnace. Then what god will be able to rescue you from my hand?"

Shadrach, Meshach and Abednego replied to him, "King Nebuchadnezzar, we do not need to defend ourselves before you in this matter. If we are thrown into the blazing furnace, the God we serve is able to deliver us from it, and he will deliver us from Your Majesty's hand. But even if he does not, we want you to know, Your Majesty, that we will not serve your gods or worship the image of gold you have set up."

Devotional

Shadrach, Meshach, and Abednego moved through their fears into an act of faith that transformed their lives and the lives of those around them. We often overestimate the size of the risks we face and underestimate the love and power of God to drive out our fears. Imagine what might happen if you could feel your fears, and then transform them in a positive direction. What might happen?

Peter Storey was a Methodist minister in Johannesburg, South Africa, from 1976 to 1994, when the struggle for South Africa's freedom from apartheid was its most intense. Storey notes that, at that time, "most clergy, black and white, some fearing the authorities, others fearing their congregations, were silent." Out of his decades of wrestling with fear and faith, he wrote:

Fear locks the door and immobilizes us. Fear imprisons the church in mediocrity and irrelevance. . . . Thank God that in spite of all the locks on all the doors, Jesus can still get into the church. He invades our places of fear and offers the gift that only he can bring: *"Peace be with you!"* . . . Jesus gives his peace—and this is going to sound so simple—by *being there*. . . . That is why we worship. . . . Oh, never, never lose that sense of simple dependence on the presence of Jesus in your life because sometimes it is all you that you will have.[44]

This story teaches us that courage is not the absence of fear but rather the capacity to step over our fears through faith in Jesus.

Question to Consider

As you consider your fears today, do Jesus' words, "Don't be afraid," come across as critical or comforting? Why?

Prayer

Lord, more often than not, I live from a place of fear rather than a place of peace and confident trust in you. Fill me with the peace you so readily offer amid the storms of life. Help me to be a non-anxious presence to those around me. In Jesus' name, amen.

Conclude with Silence (2 minutes)

DAY 4 MORNING/MIDDAY OFFICE

Silence and Stillness before God (2 minutes)

Scripture Reading: Psalm 95:1–3, 7b–8

> Come, let us sing for joy to the LORD;
>> let us shout aloud to the Rock of our salvation.
>
> Let us come before him with thanksgiving
>> and extol him with music and song.
>
> For the LORD is the great God,
>> the great King above all gods. . . .
>
> Today, if only you would hear his voice,
>> "Do not harden your hearts as you did at Meribah,
>>> as you did that day at Massah in the wilderness."

Devotional

From Genesis to Revelation, the biblical writers issue repeated calls to gratitude, calls to "come before him with thanksgiving." This giving of thanks to the living God, who is the source of all goodness in our lives, provides the antidote to our tendency to harden our hearts. This is especially true when we find ourselves in a desert experience of disappointment, suffering, or loss. As Dietrich Bonhoeffer writes:

> Only he who gives thanks for little things receives the big things. We prevent God from giving us the great spiritual

gifts he has in store for us, because we do not give thanks for daily gifts. . . . We pray for the big things and forget to give thanks for the ordinary, small (and yet really not small) gifts. How can God entrust great things to one who will not thankfully receive from him the little things?[45]

Albert Borgmann, a Christian philosopher, cuts to the heart of this lifestyle of thanksgiving in the midst of challenging times by breaking it down to four affirmations. Each serves as an antidote to the restlessness and discontent so prevalent in our day:

> There is no place I would rather be.
> There is nothing I would rather do.
> There is no one I would rather be with.
> This I will remember well.[46]

In a culture rife with entitlement and complaint, it is no small task to "Come before the Lord with thanksgiving." But if we commit to this spiritual formation practice, we find that it has the power to lead us to a new place, even to a Promised Land of great joy.

Question to Consider

Take a moment to think back over the last twenty-four hours. What "ordinary and small gifts" did God entrust to you for which you can be thankful?

Prayer

> *Father, I recognize that everything in my life is a gift from your*
> *hand, that I am completely dependent on you. Thank you for*
> *the earth, the sky, my very breath, and the work many others*
> *have done to enable me to enjoy the gift of life today. In Jesus'*
> *name, amen.*

Conclude with Silence (2 minutes)

DAY 4 MIDDAY/EVENING OFFICE

Silence and Stillness before God (2 minutes)

Scripture Reading: 1 John 4:1–3

> Dear friends, do not believe every spirit, but test the spir-
> its to see whether they are from God, because many false
> prophets have gone out into the world. This is how you can
> recognize the Spirit of God: Every spirit that acknowledges
> that Jesus Christ has come in the flesh is from God, but
> every spirit that does not acknowledge Jesus is not from
> God. This is the spirit of the antichrist, which you have
> heard is coming and even now is already in the world.

Devotional

Ignatius of Loyola (1491–1556), the founder of the Jesuits,
developed a classic discernment model that maintains a balance
between reason (intellect) and feelings (heart). He provided

excellent guidelines on how God speaks to us through our deepest feelings and yearnings, something he called "consolations" and "desolations."

Consolations are those feelings that fill us with joy, life, energy, and peace, connecting us more deeply with God. Desolations are those experiences that drain us and feel like death, disconnecting us from God, ourselves, and others.

His unique contribution was providing a structured way to acknowledge feelings as important indicators of how God reveals his will to us and how we can "test the spirits" (1 John 4:1). Within this framework, feelings are not ends in and of themselves but a means to know God and his love. Author Alice Fryling says it well:

> The goal in focusing on feelings is not to wallow in them. Nor is it just to clarify thinking. The goal is to notice and embrace the presence of God in this experience. When this happens, the peace that comes "transcends all understanding" (Philippians 4:7). In other words, we cannot *think* our way into God's peace; it's beyond understanding. The Bible also says that the love of God "surpasses knowledge" (Ephesians 3:19). No matter how much we *know*, God's love is deeper, so sometimes the route to this peace-beyond-knowing is through our feelings.[47]

This point bears repeating: the goal is not to think our way into God's will. Our task is "to notice and embrace the presence of God." And sometimes it is our feelings that lead us to peace that transcends all understanding.

Question to Consider

Briefly reflect on the events and interactions of your last twenty-four hours. Then ask yourself: When did I experience joy, peace, increased energy, or a sense of God's presence (consolation)? And when did I experience sadness, apathy, energy draining out of me, or a sense of God's absence (desolation)?

Prayer

Father, you know how easily I forget about you for hours at a time. I ask you for grace and power to pay attention and listen to you during all my waking hours. Help me to recognize your voice when you speak to me through my consolations and desolations. In Jesus' name, amen.

Conclude with Silence (2 minutes)

DAY 5 MORNING/MIDDAY OFFICE

Silence and Stillness before God (2 minutes)

Scripture Reading: Ephesians 4:25–27

Therefore each of you must put off falsehood and speak truthfully to your neighbor, for we are all members of one body. "In your anger do not sin": Do not let the sun go

down while you are still angry, and do not give the devil
a foothold.

Devotional

When we quit the lie that "good" Christians don't get angry,
we walk through a door that changes our life. Anger is a central
discipleship issue for every Christian. It is a signal alerting us to
many potential messages from God—a warning indicator light
on life's dashboard, inviting us to stop and pay attention to what
God might be saying.

Through anger, God may help us clarify our values, that is,
what we really want. When our values or beliefs are violated, we
sometimes feel it in our bodies. For example, our stomach gets
knotted, our neck tightens, we sweat, we clench our fists, our
shoulders stiffen, we can't sleep, etc. In this case, anger leads us
to action.

Anger also can lead us to deeper emotions, such as hurt,
sadness, fear, disappointment, and shame. When we are angry,
it is important to ask, "What am I afraid of? Am I hurt? Sad?
Disappointed? What is really going on beneath the anger?"

Anger may also be an indicator of unmet expectations in
relationships with family, coworkers, friends, or other believers. Then we need to discern if we actually had a right to those
expectations or if we were simply making assumptions.

Finally, anger can also be a sin, revealing our pettiness, arrogance, hatred, or envy. For this reason, integrating our anger
with our spirituality—paying attention to what God might be

saying to us through it—is a huge step to emotional and spiritual maturity.[48]

Question to Consider

As you reflect on any current or recent experiences of anger, how would you describe the "warning indicator light" or the message your anger might be trying to send you?

Prayer

> *Lord, teach me to process my anger in healthy ways that enable me to better love you, others, and myself. Help me to learn "to be angry with the right person, to the right degree, at the right time, for the right purpose, and in the right way."[49] In Jesus' name, amen.*

Conclude with Silence (2 minutes)

DAY 5 MIDDAY/EVENING OFFICE

Silence and Stillness before God (2 minutes)

Scripture Reading: Matthew 27:35–42a

> When they had crucified him, they divided up his clothes by casting lots. And sitting down, they kept watch over him there. Above his head they placed the written charge against him: THIS IS JESUS, THE KING OF THE JEWS. Two rebels were crucified with him, one on his right and one on his

left. Those who passed by hurled insults at him, shaking their heads and saying, "You who are going to destroy the temple and build it in three days, save yourself! Come down from the cross, if you are the Son of God!" In the same way the chief priests, the teachers of the law and the elders mocked him. "He saved others," they said, "but he can't save himself!"

Devotional

The crucifixion and resurrection of Jesus is the singular most important event in human history. Scandalous to Jews and foolishness to Greeks, the cross was the ultimate manifestation of the glory of God. The world's ways were condemned. The devil was dethroned and defeated. And God opened up a way, through the blood of Jesus, to a life of loving union with him. However, the arena in which we live out our relationship with God is not the prayer closet but our relationships with one another.

Author Richard Rohr has written a lovely prayer that shows us how our life with God cannot be separated from our life with others. They really are, as Jesus taught, two sides of the same coin. I invite you to read this prayer slowly, allowing each truth to inform your life and your relationships:

I thank you, Lord Jesus, for becoming a human being so
I do not have to pretend or try to be a God.

I thank you, Lord Jesus, for becoming finite and

limited so I do not have to pretend that I am infinite and limitless.

I thank you, crucified God, for becoming mortal so I do not have to try to make myself immortal.

I thank you, Lord Jesus, for becoming inferior so I do not have to pretend that I am superior to anyone. . . .

I thank you for becoming weak, so I don't have to be strong.

I thank you for being willing to be considered imperfect and strange, so I do not have to be perfect and normal.

I thank you, Lord Jesus, for being willing to be disapproved of, so I do not have to try so hard to be approved and liked.

I thank you for being considered a failure, so I do not have to give my life trying to pretend I'm a success.

I thank you for being wrong by the standards of religion and state, so I do not have to be right anywhere.

I thank you for being poor in every way, so I do not have to be rich in any way.

I thank you, Lord Jesus, for being all of the things humanity despises and fears, so I can accept myself and others in you.[50]

As Rohr says, we can be thankful for God's call for us "to die" to the manipulative and controlling ways of the world in order to embrace the crucified way of Jesus. Why? Because it is the pathway of Jesus to a life of power and resurrection.

Question to Consider

Which line in the prayer do you identify with most? Why?

Prayer

> *Lord, so much inside of me resists following you to the cross and living a life of brokenness and vulnerability. Grant me courage to follow you, all the way, whatever that might mean. In Jesus' name, amen.*

Conclude with Silence (2 minutes)

Listen
Incarnationally

DAILY OFFICES

Week Five

God became incarnate—took human form—in Jesus of Nazareth. He demonstrated his love for us by setting aside all the glory and power of his divinity so he could fully enter into our world. This act of incarnation—of setting aside rights and privileges as an act of love—is one Jesus invites us to follow. We follow him in this way any time we leave our comfort zones in order to meet people where they are.

To listen incarnationally is to enter into another person's world, at a heart level, with the empathy of Christ, attending to their nonverbal cues as well as their words. This is how we demonstrate our love for them. We truly listen to what they say and feel what they feel. And in doing so, by God's grace, they experience the presence of Christ through us.

ADDITIONAL RESOURCES

- *The Emotionally Healthy Relationships Workbook*, Session 5
- *The Emotionally Healthy Relationships DVD*, Session 5

DAY 1 MORNING/MIDDAY OFFICE

Silence and Stillness before God (2 minutes)

Scripture Reading: Matthew 25:34–36, 40

Then the King will say to those on his right, "Come, you who are blessed by my Father; take your inheritance, the kingdom prepared for you since the creation of the world. For I was hungry and you gave me something to eat, I was thirsty and you gave me something to drink, I was a stranger and you invited me in, I needed clothes and you clothed me, I was sick and you looked after me, I was in prison and you came to visit me." . . .

The King will reply, "I tell you, whatever you did for one of the least of these brothers and sisters of mine, you did for me."

Devotional

Born in the former Yugoslavia, Mother Teresa (1910–1997) joined the Sisters of Loretto in Ireland at age seventeen, and within a year was sent to Calcutta, India. There, she witnessed the profound suffering of the poor who lived and died on the streets. In 1950, she founded the Missionaries of Charity, a religious order dedicated to serving the sick and dying in the city's slums. In 1979, she won the Nobel Peace Prize for her work. By 2015, there were more than 5,600 workers serving in 844 communities around the world.[51]

Mother Teresa made no distinction between being open to the heart of Christ in prayer and being open to the hearts of others, especially the hearts of the poor. Here is how she describes what it really means to love others in Jesus' name:

It is easy to love the people far away. It is not always easy to love those close to us. It is easier to give a cup of rice to relieve hunger than to relieve the loneliness and pain of someone unloved in our own home. Bring love into your home for this is where our love for each other must start.[52]

The greatest disease in the West today is not TB [tuberculosis] or leprosy; it is being unwanted, unloved, and uncared for. We can cure physical diseases with medicine, but the only cure for loneliness, despair, and hopelessness is love. There are many in the world who are dying for a piece of bread but there are many more dying for a little love. . . .

    At the end of life we will not be judged by how many diplomas we have received, how much money we have made, how many great things we have done. We will be judged by "I was hungry and you gave me to eat. I was naked and you clothed me. I was homeless and you took me in."[53]

And Mother Teresa, in following the way of Christ by loving one person at a time, changed the world.

Question to Consider

What phrases or sentences from these Mother Teresa quotes most speak to you today?

Prayer

> *Lord, forgive me for the times I have ignored your voice and avoided entering into the pain or loneliness of those you have placed around me, especially those closest to me. Help me to really see the needs of those around me today—and then to listen. Then may the words and actions that flow from me reflect your heart of love. In Jesus' name, amen.*

Conclude with Silence (2 minutes)

DAY 1 MIDDAY/EVENING OFFICE

Silence and Stillness before God (2 minutes)

Scripture Reading: Isaiah 49:14–16

> But Zion said, "The LORD has forsaken me,
>> the Lord has forgotten me."
> "Can a mother forget the baby at her breast
>> and have no compassion on the child she has borne?
> Though she may forget,
>> I will not forget you!
> See, I have engraved you on the palms of my hands;
>> your walls are ever before me."

Devotional

In this passage, we are given two beautiful images of the infinite love God has for us. He refers to himself first as a nursing mother who cannot forget us. He then says we are permanently tattooed on his hands. Think about that! We are always on God's mind, permanently inked into his very being. In spite of our faults, sins, and mistakes, God is crazy in love with us!

As much as he loves us, God knows we also need to experience his love through other human beings. German philosopher Josef Pieper (1904–1997) writes compellingly about the powerful connection between God's love and the love of another person:

> It does not suffice to us simply to exist; we can do that anyhow. What matters to us, beyond mere existence, is the explicit confirmation: It is *good* that you exist; how wonderful that you are! In other words, what we need over and above sheer existence is: to be loved by another person. That is an astonishing fact when we consider it closely. Being created by God actually does not suffice, it would seem; the fact of creation needs continuation and perfection by the creative power of human love. . . .
>
> We say that a person "blossoms" when undergoing the experience of being loved; that he becomes wholly himself for the first time; that a "new life" is beginning for him . . . a man succeeds in fully existing and feeling at home in the world only when he is "being confirmed" by the love of another.[54]

When people were with Jesus, they thrived, sensing these words from his very presence: "It is *good* that you exist; how wonderful that you are!" Allow yourself to receive the gift of that message from him now.

Question to Consider

Recognizing that "a person blossoms when undergoing the experience of being loved," who is one person you can help to blossom this week by intentionally offering them the experience of being loved?

Prayer

Father, thank you that my name is permanently engraved on your hands and that you love me even more than a mother loves her newborn. Help me to rest in this deep love so that loving the people around me becomes my first instinct and natural response. In Jesus' name, amen.

Silence and Stillness before God (2 minutes)

DAY 2 MORNING/MIDDAY OFFICE

Silence and Stillness before God (2 minutes)

Scripture Reading: Luke 5:12–13

While Jesus was in one of the towns, a man came along who was covered with leprosy. When he saw Jesus, he fell

with his face to the ground and begged him, "Lord, if you
are willing, you can make me clean."

Jesus reached out his hand and touched the man. "I am
willing," he said. "Be clean!" And immediately the leprosy
left him.

Devotional

Jesus' presence had a healing and transformative impact on
people—physically, spiritually, and emotionally. As we become
more like him, more rooted and established in his love, our
presence can impact people as well.

Martin Buber (1878–1965), a German-Jewish philosopher
and author, explores this profound principle in his classic book,
I and Thou. The book was first published in 1923, just five years
after the end of World War I.

Before the war began, Buber considered the "religious" to be
mystical experiences that lifted him out of the earthly, ordinary
experiences of everyday life. He was more concerned with the
eternal than with the temporal, more focused on ecstasy than
daily existence, more interested in what lies beyond the world
than in the world itself.[55]

That all changed one day in 1914, the year that World War
I broke out in Europe, when a young man came to visit Buber.

What happened was no more than that one forenoon, after
a morning of "religious" enthusiasm, I had a visit from
an unknown young man, without being there in spirit.

I certainly did not fail to let the meeting be friendly. . . .
I conversed attentively and openly with him—only I omit-
ted to guess the questions which he did not put. Later, not
long after, I learned from one of his friends—he himself was
no longer alive—the essential content of these questions;
I learned that he had come to me not casually, but borne
by destiny, not for a chat but for a decision. He had come
to me, he had come in this hour.[56]

The young man had committed suicide. The guilt Buber
felt was not that he had somehow failed to remove the young
man's despair, but that he was not fully present to him. He was
so preoccupied by his religious experience earlier that morning,
that he failed to bring the full resources of his attention to
their conversation. He did not turn to the young man with
his whole being to actually *feel with* him. Instead of genuinely listening, he brought leftovers, a courteous but partial
engagement.

For Buber, the experience felt like a judgment on his whole
way of life.[57] He realized that it is possible to have profound
spiritual experiences and a "faith that can move mountains,"
but that such a faith is worth nothing without a deeply present
love for people.

Question to Consider

What would you say is your greatest obstacle or challenge to
being fully present and engaged with others?

Prayer

> *Father, I am so easily distracted and preoccupied when I am*
> *with people, but I long to be the kind of person who genuinely*
> *listens and is fully present. I ask that you would change me*
> *so that I can be a transformative presence for others. In Jesus'*
> *name, amen.*

Conclude with Silence (2 minutes)

DAY 2 MIDDAY/EVENING OFFICE

Silence and Stillness before God (2 minutes)

Scripture Reading: Luke 7:11–17

Soon afterward, Jesus went to a town called Nain, and his
disciples and a large crowd went along with him. As he
approached the town gate, a dead person was being carried
out—the only son of his mother, and she was a widow. And
a large crowd from the town was with her. When the Lord
saw her, his heart went out to her and he said, "Don't cry."

Then he went up and touched the bier they were carrying him on, and the bearers stood still. He said, "Young
man, I say to you, get up!" The dead man sat up and began
to talk, and Jesus gave him back to his mother.

They were all filled with awe and praised God. "A great
prophet has appeared among us," they said. "God has come

to help his people." This news about Jesus spread throughout Judea and the surrounding country.

Devotional

The gospels are filled with accounts of Jesus' interactions with individuals—Matthew, Nathaniel, a prostitute, Nicodemus, a blind man, a Samaritan woman, and many others. When a rich young ruler came up to him, Jesus "looked at him and loved him." He listened. He was present, never in a rush or distracted. He gave people the dignity of listening to their stories.

When is the last time you heard someone say something like this: "Those Christians are fantastic listeners! I have never known a group of people who are so genuinely interested in my world, so good at asking questions, and so attentive"?

When we choose to enter into the world of another person, we are choosing to be available and present. Jesus did not return the boy of Nain to his widowed mother without first having been present to her in her sorrow. In doing so, he modeled a relationship of care and loving presence. Here is how author Henri Nouwen describes such love and care:

> From experience, you know that those who care for you become present to you. When they listen, they listen to you. When they speak, you know they speak to you. And when they ask questions, you know it is for your sake and not their own. Their presence is a healing presence because

they accept you on your terms, and they encourage you to take your own life seriously.[58]

In the same way, God invites us to grow in the quality of our presence to others so that they might experience his love through us.

Question to Consider

In what way(s) are you tempted to be distracted when you are with people rather than be present, deeply listening and accepting them on their own terms?

Prayer

> *Lord, teach me by the Holy Spirit to listen deeply to the people I am with today, to see them as you see them, and to love them as you love them. In Jesus' name, amen.*

Conclude with Silence (2 minutes)

DAY 3 MORNING/MIDDAY OFFICE

Silence and Stillness before God (2 minutes)

Scripture Reading: John 13:34–35

> A new command I give you: Love one another. As I have loved you, so you must love one another. By this everyone will know that you are my disciples, if you love one another.

Devotional

Jewish theologian Martin Buber argued that in most of our routine interactions we tend to treat people as objects or means to an end, which he described as "I-It" relationships. However, the healthiest or most mature relationships between human beings are those Buber characterized as "I-Thou" relationships.

These true relationships, said Buber, can exist only between two people willing to connect across their differences. God fills that in-between space of an I-Thou relationship. God not only can be glimpsed in genuine dialogue between the two persons, but also penetrates the space between them, making it sacred space:

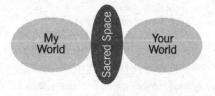

The central tenet of Buber's life work was that the I-Thou relationship between persons intimately reflects the I-Thou relationship humans have with God. Genuine relationship with any Thou shows traces of the "eternal Thou." This helps to explain why it is a powerful experience when we listen deeply to someone. When genuine love is found in a relationship, God's presence is manifest. The space that once separated us becomes sacred space.[59]

Question to Consider

What adjustments might you need to make to treat each person you meet today as a "Thou" rather than an "It"?

Prayer

> *Lord, help me slow down so that I don't treat people as objects*
> *or obstacles to be overcome. Thank you that you always treat*
> *me as a Thou. With your help, I want to do the same for others*
> *this day. In Jesus' name, amen.*

Conclude with Silence (2 minutes)

DAY 3 MIDDAY/EVENING OFFICE

Silence and Stillness before God (2 minutes)

Scripture Reading: 1 Corinthians 13:1–3

> If I speak in the tongues of men or of angels, but do not have
> love, I am only a resounding gong or a clanging cymbal. If
> I have the gift of prophecy and can fathom all mysteries
> and all knowledge, and if I have a faith that can move
> mountains, but do not have love, I am nothing. If I give all
> I possess to the poor and give over my body to hardship that
> I may boast, but do not have love, I gain nothing.

Devotional

This passage makes an astounding claim: It is possible to operate in the power of the Spirit through miracles and spiritual
gifts and not be a Christian. You can build a great ministry for
God—doing miracles, sacrificing everything you have, and using
spiritual gifts—and not be a real follower of Jesus Christ at all.

In fact, the apostle Paul goes so far as to call all these actions "nothing."

Perhaps even more astonishing, it appears that the level of spiritual power and gifting operating through a believer's life may have little to do with spiritual maturity. Spiritual gifts can operate through us even when we remain spiritual infants. According to Paul, the only true sign of the Spirit at work is supernatural love, not gifts or even "successful" results.

Love is the only accomplishment on earth that will last forever. In heaven, we will love each other perfectly, utterly, and without any limits. When we live out this *agape* (unconditional) love on earth, we are experiencing the authentic kingdom of God. We taste heaven.

Jonathan Edwards (1703–1758), one of America's best-known theologians and preachers, offers us this beautiful description of what heaven will be like:

> Heaven [is] a world of love; for God is the fountain of love, as the sun is the fountain of light. And therefore the glorious presence of God in heaven, fills heaven with love, as the sun, placed in the midst of the visible heavens in a clear day, fills the world with light. The apostle tells us that "God is love;" and therefore, seeing he is an infinite being, it follows that he is an infinite fountain of love.[60]

The purpose of the Christian life, therefore, is not about doing more things for God, "fixing" people, or even making the world a better place. It is simply to love people the way God loves us, to give everyone we encounter a taste of heaven on earth.

Question to Consider

What might be one practical way you can slow down in order to love someone in the next twenty-four hours?

Prayer

> *Lord, I ask you to do a supernatural work of grace in my heart so that I might love people like you do. Grant me the grace to be patient and kind, not envious or proud, filling me with the water that overflows from your infinite fountain of love. In Jesus' name, amen.*

Conclude with Silence (2 minutes)

DAY 4 MORNING/MIDDAY OFFICE

Silence and Stillness before God (2 minutes)

Scripture Reading: Job 2:11; 42:7–8

> When Job's three friends, Eliphaz the Temanite, Bildad the Shuhite and Zophar the Naamathite, heard about all the troubles that had come upon him, they set out from their homes and met together by agreement to go and sympathize with him and comfort him. . . .
>
> After the LORD had said these things to Job, he said

to Eliphaz the Temanite, "I am angry with you and your two friends, because you have not spoken the truth about me, as my servant Job has. So now take seven bulls and seven rams and go to my servant Job and sacrifice a burnt offering for yourselves. My servant Job will pray for you, and I will accept his prayer and not deal with you according to your folly. You have not spoken the truth about me, as my servant Job has."

Devotional

The book of Job is not merely a book about undeserved suffering. It is also a book about friends who don't listen. Job's friends started off well enough by being silent, and sitting with Job for seven days. But then they started talking—a lot. And that's when they got into trouble. In fact, not only did they not listen, but they went on jabbering for thirty-four chapters. They gave bad counsel, wrongly quoted Scripture, and put words in God's mouth.

Author Eugene Peterson aptly summarizes the impact of friends like Job's:

The moment we find ourselves in trouble of any kind . . . people start showing up telling us exactly what is wrong with us and what we must do to get better. . . .

It all sounds so hopeful. But then we begin to wonder, "Why is it that for all their apparent compassion we feel worse instead of better when they've said their piece?"

The book of Job is not only a witness to the dignity of suffering and God's presence in our suffering but is also our primary biblical protest against religion that has been reduced to explanations or "answers."[61]

More often than not, most of us err on the side of speaking too much. And that's when we get into trouble. The author of Ecclesiastes reminds us, "[There is] a time to be silent and a time to speak" (Ecclesiastes 3:7). The key is to discern the difference.

Question to Consider

With whom might God be inviting you to be a more humble, attentive listener today?

Prayer

Lord, free me from the need to "say something," especially when I just want to appear right or wise or impressive. Teach me to be comfortable with the powerlessness I often feel when I listen without providing answers. Protect me from foolishly talking too much, and help me become a better lover of others. In Jesus' name, amen.

Conclude with Silence (2 minutes)

DAY 4 MIDDAY/EVENING OFFICE

Silence and Stillness before God (2 minutes)

Scripture Reading: Deuteronomy 32:10–11

> In a desert land he found him,
>> in a barren and howling waste.
> He shielded him and cared for him;
>> he guarded him as the apple of his eye,
> like an eagle that stirs up its nest
>> and hovers over its young,
> that spreads its wings to catch them
>> and carries them aloft.

Devotional

In this beautiful passage, God compares himself to a mother eagle who stirs up her eaglets to leave the nest in order to fly. Just as the mother eagle protects and supports her young by hovering beneath them with her wings, so God flies beneath us with his powerful wings to catch and carry us.

When author and educator Parker Palmer describes the Quaker process of a creating a safe space for individuals to get "clearness" about where God's Spirit might be leading them, he compares it to holding that person like a small bird in the palm of our hands. He notes, however, that there are great temptations for us as listeners.

I suggest, we are to hold the soul of the focus person as if we were holding a small bird in the palms of our two hands.

As we do so, we are likely to experience three temptations, and it is important that we resist all of them:

- After a while, our hands may start to close around the bird, wanting to take this creature apart and find out what makes it tick. Resist this temptation. . . .

- As the time goes by, our arms may begin to tire, and we may find ourselves tempted to lay the bird down: attention flags, the mind wanders. . . . We must resist this temptation too. A bird is light, and a soul is even lighter. . . .

- Toward the end of the process . . . we may find our cupped hands making a subtle but persistent upward motion, encouraging the bird to fly: . . . "Aren't you ready to take off, to act on what you now know?" Resist this temptation too. This bird will fly when it is ready, and we cannot possibly know when that will be.[62]

When listening, we often feel a great temptation to rush God's process or manipulate outcomes. We need to remember that it is God—not us—who is responsible for nudging his children out of the nest. The timing is up to him. Our role is to love, to listen, and to cooperate with what his Spirit is doing in the life of the person we are listening to.

Question to Consider

As you anticipate spending time with someone today, what difference might it make in your ability to listen well if you could imagine holding that person like a small bird in the palm of your hands?

Prayer

Father, thank you that you are a God who always listens to me. Help me to trust you as I listen to others, holding them gently—not rushing to fix them, save them, or hurry them along their journey with you. Help me to trust your timetable and your work in their lives. In Jesus' name, amen.

Conclude with Silence (2 minutes)

DAY 5 MORNING/MIDDAY OFFICE

Silence and Stillness before God (2 minutes)

Scripture Reading: John 11:32–36, 40

When Mary reached the place where Jesus was and saw him, she fell at his feet and said, "Lord, if you had been here, my brother would not have died."

When Jesus saw her weeping, and the Jews who had come along with her also weeping, he was deeply moved in spirit and troubled. "Where have you laid him?" he asked.

"Come and see, Lord," they replied.

Jesus wept.

Then the Jews said, "See how he loved him!" . . .

Then Jesus said, "Did I not tell you that if you believe, you will see the glory of God?"

Devotional

In this passage, we catch a powerful glimpse of Jesus deeply moved, troubled in spirit, and shedding real tears. Without holding anything back, he enters into Mary's pain and looks straight into the devastation of Lazarus's death. By watching Jesus at the gravesite, we learn a crucial lesson about loving people. Henri Nouwen describes it well:

> No one can help anyone without becoming involved, without entering with his whole person into the painful situation, without taking the risk of becoming hurt, wounded or even destroyed in the process. . . . [R]eal martyrdom means a witness that starts with the willingness to cry with those who cry, laugh with those who laugh, and to make one's own painful and joyful experiences available as sources of clarification and understanding.
>
> Who can save a child from a burning house without taking the risk of being hurt by the flames? Who can listen to a story of loneliness and despair without taking the risk of experiencing similar pains in his own heart and even losing his precious peace of mind? In short: "Who can take away suffering without entering it?"
>
> The great illusion of leadership is to think that man can be led out of the desert by someone who has never been there.[63]

Nouwen's question is a sobering one: "Who can take away suffering without entering it?" Yet, as Jesus taught, it is only

when we lose our lives for others that we truly find them
(Mark 8:35).

Question to Consider

Jesus acknowledged a promise when he said, "Did I not tell you
that if you believe, you will see the glory of God?" How might
this promise encourage you to step over your fears and listen to
the pain of others today?

Prayer

> *Lord, so often I pull back from really listening to the pains of
> other people, fearing their problems might swallow me up. You
> modeled an ability to enter into the "loneliness and despair"
> of others while still remaining separate and centered in the
> Father. Teach me to enter into the pain of others as willingly
> as you did, remembering both my limits and that you are God,
> not me. In Jesus' name, amen.*

Conclude with Silence (2 minutes)

DAY 5 MIDDAY/EVENING OFFICE

Silence and Stillness before God (2 minutes)

Scripture Reading: Luke 8:5–8

> "A farmer went out to sow his seed. As he was scattering the
> seed, some fell along the path; it was trampled on, and the

birds ate it up. Some fell on rocky ground, and when it came up, the plants withered because they had no moisture. Other seed fell among thorns, which grew up with it and choked the plants. Still other seed fell on good soil. It came up and yielded a crop, a hundred times more than was sown."

When he said this, he called out, "Whoever has ears to hear, let them hear."

Devotional

The key to understanding Jesus' parable of the Sower are his final words, "Whoever has ears to hear, let them hear." Jesus wants us to know God is sowing his Word in the world and the most important posture we can have in life is that of attentive listening. Disciples who are good soil pay attention to him, yielding fruit a hundredfold. Believers represented by the other three soils—the well-trodden path, the rocky ground, the thorn-choked patch—do not. They are distracted and inattentive.

Leighton Ford, a renowned Christian leader and writer, sums up the indispensability of attentive listening to God this way:

Attentiveness is one of the most difficult concepts to grasp and one of the hardest disciplines to learn. For we are a very distractible people in a very distracting world.

God wants us to be an attentive people, as he is an attentive God. Many of the words of God in the Bible call his people to "look," "see," "listen," "give heed." . . .

The influential French writer Simone Weil believed that attention was at the very heart of prayer, and her French forbear Blaise Pascal also felt that inattention is the greatest enemy of the spiritual life. . . . Attentiveness, as I have come to see, is most critical for us to find the way to clarity of heart, and clarity is the path to seeing God, who is the source and end of all our longing.[64]

Do you see now why distractibility and inattention are such great enemies of the spiritual life? When we fail to listen to God, to tune our hearts for his faintest whisper, we are risking nothing less than the substance of our spiritual life as well as our most important relationships.

Question to Consider

What is one practical step you can take today to lessen your distractibility and offer a deeper, more sustained focus to God and to the people around you?

Prayer

Lord, I recognize I am a distracted person. Help me to let go of my need to keep up with everything happening around me, and to trust you with the world. Please strengthen my ability to pay attention to you and to the people around me so I can love them as you love them. In Jesus' name, amen.

Conclude with Silence (2 minutes)

Climb the Ladder
of Integrity

Reflecting on our values, our feelings, and our thoughts, especially in the presence of God, is holy work. It is also hard work. But as we do so, prayerfully sifting the inner movements of our heart by the Spirit, we discern more clearly what is and is not from God. Then, instead of reacting defensively or blaming others, we respond lovingly out of our God-given self.

The Ladder of Integrity is a step-by-step process to help us do just that—to clarify our values and to be honest and clear about what is going on inside us. When we do this, we have integrity—what is important to us on the inside becomes how we live on the outside. We are then able to offer the world the love of Jesus without impediment.

ADDITIONAL RESOURCES

- *The Emotionally Healthy Relationships Workbook*, Session 6
- *The Emotionally Healthy Relationships DVD*, Session 6

DAY 1 MORNING/MIDDAY OFFICE

Silence and Stillness before God (2 minutes)

Scripture Reading: Matthew 16:21–23

> From that time on Jesus began to explain to his disciples that
> he must go to Jerusalem and suffer many things at the hands
> of the elders, the chief priests and the teachers of the law, and
> that he must be killed and on the third day be raised to life.
>
> Peter took him aside and began to rebuke him. "Never,
> Lord!" he said. "This shall never happen to you!"
>
> Jesus turned and said to Peter, "Get behind me, Satan!
> You are a stumbling block to me; you do not have in mind
> the concerns of God, but merely human concerns."

Devotional

Many of us feel guilty saying no. We want to be liked and not
disappoint people, and we perhaps imagine that saying no is
somehow less than Christlike. But consider Jesus' example and
whether or not he disappointed people by sometimes saying no.

- He said no to the crowds who wanted to make him king
  (John 6:14–16).
- He said no to Peter who wanted him to avoid the cross
  (Matthew 16:21–23).
- He said no to the religious leaders who wanted him to
  stop claiming to be the Messiah (John 5:16–18).

- He said no to his family who wanted him to return home (Mark 3:31–34).
- He said no to the people who wanted him to come down off the cross to prove he was the Son of God (Luke 23:35–39).

If Jesus had refused to say no for fear of disappointing people, he would not have fulfilled the mission and the purpose God gave him. He would have lived up to other people's expectations instead of his own. And the same is true for us. Exercising a healthy no is essential if we are to fulfill the Father's destiny for our lives.

It's important to understand that both *yes* and *no* are loving words. Remember, when I say no, it is not *against* you but *for* me. And while my no may make you sad, it doesn't make me bad. Most importantly, if I say yes when what I really want to say is no, I erode my integrity and hurt both of us. We must be able to say no if we are to say a healthy yes.[65]

Question to Consider

Under what circumstance, or to whom, do you find it difficult to say no? Why?

Prayer

Lord, I need your power and wisdom to live courageously and to say an empowered and healthy yes or no when appropriate. Free me from the fear of disappointing people so that I can live the life of purpose and integrity you have destined me to live. In Jesus' name, amen.

Conclude with Silence (2 minutes)

DAY 1 MIDDAY/EVENING OFFICE

Silence and Stillness before God (2 minutes)

Scripture Reading: John 1:19–23

Now this was John's testimony when the Jewish leaders in Jerusalem sent priests and Levites to ask him *who he was*. He did not fail to confess, but confessed freely, "I am not the Messiah."

They asked him, "*Then who are you?* Are you Elijah?"

He said, "I am not."

"Are you the Prophet?"

He answered, "No."

Finally they said, "*Who are you?* Give us an answer to take back to those who sent us. What do you say about yourself?"

John replied in the words of Isaiah the prophet, "I am the voice of one calling in the wilderness, 'Make straight the way for the Lord.'" (emphasis added)

Devotional

John the Baptist clearly knows who he is and who he is not. The clarity he has about his identity and his role positions him to bear a powerful witness to Jesus and his kingdom.

When John the Baptist states three times that he is not the Messiah, it does not mean he thinks he is a nobody. He honestly believes, and so publicly affirms, that he is the one called "a voice" predicted by Isaiah to prepare the Way of the Lord. Biblical scholar Frederick Dale Bruner writes, "It is almost as if he is saying, 'I don't know many things about myself and my calling, but I do know one thing: I was sent into history to bring people to a place where they would willingly be immersed in water to show their true repentance.'"[66]

Just as John the Baptist was clear, it is critically important that we assess and affirm the "I am" and the "I am not'" of our own identity. This provides us with a healthy, clearly defined understanding of our gifts and limits.

Consider author Fredrick Buechner's contribution to this discernment process of gaining greater clarity about ourselves over time:

> There are all different kinds of voices calling you to all different kinds of work, and the problem is to find out which is the voice of God rather than of society.
>
> By and large, a good rule for finding out is this: The kind of work God usually calls you to is the kind of work (a) you most need to do and (b) that the world most needs to have done. . . . The place God calls you to is the place your deep gladness and the world's deep hunger meet.[67]

Then, as a result of hearing God's voice more clearly, we can move into the world more faithfully to bear witness to Jesus and his kingdom.

Question to Consider

What comes to mind when you consider where your "deep gladness" meets the world's "deep hunger"?

Prayer

> *Father, so many people and voices are pulling me in different directions that it is hard to imagine enjoying the kind of clarity John the Baptist had about his life. Teach me to be better attuned to your voice. And lead me continually on the unique path you have laid out for me. In Jesus' name, amen.*

Conclude with Silence (2 minutes)

DAY 2 MORNING/MIDDAY OFFICE

Silence and Stillness before God (2 minutes)

Scripture Reading: John 3:25–29a

> An argument developed between some of John's disciples and a certain Jew over the matter of ceremonial washing. They came to John and said to him, "Rabbi, that man who was with you on the other side of the Jordan—the one you testified about—look, he is baptizing, and everyone is going to him."
>
> To this John replied, "A person can receive only what is given them from heaven. You yourselves can testify that I said, 'I am not the Messiah but am sent ahead of him.' The bride belongs to the bridegroom."

Devotional

John the Baptist exhibited great courage and integrity in embracing his God-given purpose despite the pressure all around him. He was clear that "a person can receive only what is given them from heaven" (John 3:27). God invites us to live with a similar integrity, even when we pay a price for doing so. Civil rights pioneer Rosa Parks offers a stunning example of this.

Rosa Parks was an African-American woman living in the segregated South in the 1950s. She was tired of pretending everything was fine when it was not. Author Parker Palmer describes what became a history-changing moment—both for her and the Civil Rights movement:

> On December 1, 1955, in Montgomery, Alabama, Rosa Parks did something she was not supposed to do: she sat down at the front of a bus in one of the seats reserved for whites—a dangerous, daring, and provocative act in a racist society....
>
> [When] asked, "Why did you sit down at the front of the bus that day?" Rosa Parks did not say that she sat down to launch a movement.... She said, "I sat down because I was tired." But she did not mean that her feet were tired. She meant that her soul was tired, her heart was tired, her whole being was tired of playing by racist rules, of denying her soul's claim to selfhood.[68]

Rosa Parks made a decision that day to no longer live divided. She would no longer submit on the outside to laws and to a culture that contradicted the truth of her integrity on the inside.

God invites us to live divided no more as well. When we do, we—and ultimately everyone around us—experience a newfound freedom.[69]

Question to Consider

Here are some signs that we are living a divided life, a life without integrity:

- We care too much what others think.
- We spin the truth, exaggerate, or lie to make ourselves look better.
- We blame others rather than take responsibility for our words and actions.
- We avoid confrontation.
- We say yes when we prefer to say no.

Which of these characteristics, if any, might be true of you? What makes it difficult for you to live with integrity in this area of life?

Prayer

Father, I want to live out of my true self, to live undivided. I ask that you fill me with the same supernatural power that raised Jesus from the dead so that I can make even a small "Rosa Parks" decision today—a decision to not pretend everything is fine when it is not. In Jesus' name, amen.

Conclude with Silence (2 minutes)

DAY 2 MIDDAY/EVENING OFFICE

Silence and Stillness before God (2 minutes)

Scripture Reading: Exodus 3:1–5

Now Moses was tending the flock of Jethro his father-in-law, the priest of Midian, and he led the flock to the far side of the wilderness and came to Horeb, the mountain of God. There the angel of the LORD appeared to him in flames of fire from within a bush. Moses saw that though the bush was on fire it did not burn up. So Moses thought, "I will go over and see this strange sight—why the bush does not burn up."

When the LORD saw that he had gone over to look, God called to him from within the bush, "Moses! Moses!"

And Moses said, "Here I am."

"Do not come any closer," God said. "Take off your sandals, for the place where you are standing is holy ground."

Devotional

At the age of eighty, Moses heard God's voice in a very unlikely place, and it changed his destiny. One minute he was an obscure desert shepherd. The next moment, God invited him to overcome enormous obstacles (everything from his past failures to the all-powerful Pharaoh) in order to set the Israelites free from 400 years of slavery.

God's voice often comes to us in similar ways. In unlikely events and circumstances, he calls us to listen to him, allowing him to interrupt our lives, and lead us to new places. It was an uncomfortable experience for Moses, and it is no less uncomfortable for us. That's almost always what it feels like when we take a risk to follow God into the unknown. It's an experience not all that different from the one faced by test pilot Chuck Yeager, the first human being to break the sound barrier.

The year was 1947, and nobody had ever surpassed the speed of sound—760 mph at sea level—due to a widely held belief in the existence of a "sound barrier," an invisible wall of air that would smash an airplane that tried to pierce it.

When Chuck Yeager was invited to be the test pilot, his boss informed him, "Nobody knows for sure what happens until somebody gets there. Chuck, you'll be flying into the unknown."[70] Neither the Air Force nor the colonel could guarantee the outcome. Nobody had been there before.

After nine attempts, on October 14, 1947, Yeager finally broke the sound barrier. He wrote later about the experience, "I was thunderstruck. After all the anxiety, breaking the sound barrier turned out to be a perfectly paved speedway. . . . After all the anticipation it was really a let down. The 'unknown' was a poke through Jell-O."[71]

You may be wondering what will happen if you take seriously God's purpose for you and allow him to lead you to new places. Yes, your life, like Yeager's airplane, will shake in the process of you maturing into the person God intends. But if you move forward, you will find that God is with you and behind you. And the terrifying unknown ahead may well turn out to be no more frightening than "a poke through Jell-O."

Question to Consider

How has God been seeking to get your attention lately? What is your "burning bush" equivalent—that issue that is burning but won't die?

Prayer

Lord Jesus, set me free to be the person you have created me to be, and to do what you have called me to do. Like Moses, I ask you to help me to leave behind the negative experiences and failures of the past so that I can follow you into the future you have for me. Help me discern your hand at work in and through every circumstance and season of my life. In Jesus' name, amen.

Conclude with Silence (2 minutes)

DAY 3 MORNING/MIDDAY OFFICE

Silence and Stillness before God (2 minutes)

Scripture Reading: Luke 22:39–44

Jesus went out as usual to the Mount of Olives, and his disciples followed him. On reaching the place, he said to

them, "Pray that you will not fall into temptation." He
withdrew about a stone's throw beyond them, knelt down
and prayed, "Father, if you are willing, take this cup from
me; yet not my will, but yours be done."

An angel from heaven appeared to him and strength-
ened him. And being in anguish, he prayed more earnestly,
and his sweat was like drops of blood falling to the ground.

Devotional

Until this point in his earthly life, Jesus had predicted that his
calling was to suffer God's judgment for the sins of humanity by
means of an awful death on the cross. But here in Gethsamane
he struggles with the horror of drinking this particular cup of
suffering. He prays, he wrestles, and then submits to the Father's
will for his life. In doing so, Jesus models the profound surrender
required of every believer.

God has a cup of suffering for each of us to drink—our
unique, God-given destiny. It involves limits, setbacks, and difficult choices. Henri Nouwen summarizes this experience well:

No two lives are the same. We often compare our lives with
those of others, trying to decide whether we are better or
worse off, but such comparisons do not help us much. We
have to live our life, not someone else's. We have to hold *our
own* cup. We have to dare to say: "This is my life, the life
that is given to me, and it is this life that I have to live, as
well as I can. My life is unique. Nobody else will ever live

it. I have my own history, my own family, my own body, my own character, my own friends, my own way of thinking, speaking, and acting—yes, I have my own life to live. No one else has the same challenge. I am alone, because I am unique. Many people can help me live my life, but after all is said and done, I have to make my own choices about how to live."[72]

Most of us don't have a problem with doing God's will—as long as it doesn't involve too much pain. The reality, however, is that we all have particular struggles and vulnerabilities that tempt us to stray from the center of God's will.

Question to Consider

How might today be different if, instead of comparing your life to others or trying to avoid your "cup," you surrendered yourself to it?

Prayer

Lord, thank you for crafting a unique and unrepeatable life for me to live. Forgive me for how often I have strayed from that path and compared my life to those of others. Fill me with the Holy Spirit, and grant me wisdom, power, and the courage to follow you—even when I am not sure where or how you are leading me. In Jesus' name, amen.

Conclude with Silence (2 minutes)

DAY 3 MIDDAY/EVENING OFFICE

Silence and Stillness before God (2 minutes)

Scripture Reading: Daniel 1:3–5, 8

Then the king ordered Ashpenaz, chief of his court officials, to bring into the king's service some of the Israelites from the royal family and the nobility—young men without any physical defect, handsome, showing aptitude for every kind of learning, well informed, quick to understand, and qualified to serve in the king's palace. He was to teach them the language and literature of the Babylonians. The king assigned them a daily amount of food and wine from the king's table. They were to be trained for three years, and after that they were to enter the king's service. . . .

But Daniel resolved not to defile himself with the royal food and wine, and he asked the chief official for permission not to defile himself this way.

Devotional

Nebuchadnezzar and his Babylonian armies, with their gods, conquered Jerusalem and carried off most of the city's inhabitants as slaves. One of those was a young teenager named Daniel. Cut off from his family, teachers, friends, food, culture, and language, Daniel was brought into the Babylonian court and sent to the best university in the land. There he was forced to study a pagan way of viewing the world—including myths, astrology, sorcery, and magic, all of which were banned in Israel. In an effort to assimilate Daniel, the Babylonians even changed his name. He would now be called Belteshazzar.

The king of Babylon had one simple goal: to eliminate Daniel's distinctiveness as a God follower and absorb him into the values of their culture. Yet, Daniel resisted the enormous power of Babylon. He remained reflective and prayerful, not leaving the issue of his interior life or his integrity to chance.

While we know little of the specifics, it's clear that Daniel oriented his entire life around loving God. He renounced certain activities, such as eating the king's food, and engaged in others, such as daily prayer. Despite the hostile environment in which he found himself, Daniel not only fed himself spiritually, but he kept his integrity and blossomed into an extraordinary man of God.

Question to Consider

In what areas of your life (values, attitudes, activities, lifestyle choices, etc.) might God be calling you to follow Daniel—to resist the values of the culture?

Prayer

Lord, I need vision and courage to approach my relationships like Daniel, especially at work and home. Rather than just passively going along with the crowd, help me to live what I believe—to speak and to act with integrity. In Jesus' name, amen.

Conclude with Silence (2 minutes)

DAY 4 MORNING/MIDDAY OFFICE

Silence and Stillness before God (2 minutes)

Scripture Reading: Genesis 3:4–7

> "You will not certainly die," the serpent said to the woman.
> "For God knows that when you eat from [the tree] your
> eyes will be opened, and you will be like God, knowing
> good and evil."
>
> When the woman saw that the fruit of the tree was
> good for food and pleasing to the eye, and also desirable for
> gaining wisdom, she took some and ate it. She also gave some
> to her husband, who was with her, and he ate it. Then the
> eyes of both of them were opened, and they realized they
> were naked; so they sewed fig leaves together and made
> coverings for themselves.

Devotional

After Adam and Eve turned away from God, they used fig leaves
to cover and hide their shame. These fig leaves have often been
referred to by spiritual writers as the false or idealized selves we
project in the world to cover and hide the shame we feel about
our true selves. We effectively put on a fig leaf whenever we tie
our identity to anything but the deep love of God and his will
for our lives. Theologian Robert Mulholland identifies a few of
the elusive qualities of such a false self:

When we live as a false self we fear that our lack of a true center for our identity will be revealed and that weakness exploited by others. One of the ways our false self tries to compensate is to find our identity in performance. "I am what I do" is one of primal perspectives of the false self....

Our false self is a master manipulator, always seeking to leverage its world and all those in it in ways most advantageous to our own security, prestige and especially, agenda.... Our false self always promotes us and our agenda above all others....

The worst form of the false self is when it gets religion, when it becomes a religious false self.... [It] develops so gradually over the years of our life—it is so subtly ingrained into us by our culture—that we usually are not even aware of its presence.[73]

All our relationships are impacted negatively when we live out of a false self, when we choose to project and protect an idealized image. They are also impacted positively when we live out of a true self anchored and grounded in God. God invites us to trust him as we go out into the world, noticing with whom we may be wearing a false self, and trusting that he will take care of us if we live truthfully and authentically.

Question to Consider

As you consider taking off any "fig leaves" you may be wearing, how do you hear God's promises, "Do not fear. I love you. I will never leave you"?

Prayer

> *Lord, grant me courage to see where I am hiding behind the fig leaves of a false self that is afraid of being exposed. Help me to trust your love and to let it fill every part of my being. In Jesus' name, amen.*

Conclude with Silence (2 minutes)

DAY 4 MIDDAY/EVENING OFFICE

Silence and Stillness before God (2 minutes)

Scripture Reading: Numbers 11:10–12, 14–15, 17–18, 20–23

Moses heard the people of every family wailing . . . and Moses was troubled. He asked the LORD, "Why have you brought this trouble on your servant? What have I done to displease you that you put the burden of all these people on me? . . . I cannot carry all these people by myself; the burden is too heavy for me. If this is how you are going to treat me, please go ahead and kill me—if I have found favor in your eyes—and do not let me face my own ruin." . . .

[God said,] "I will take some of the power of the Spirit that is on you and put it on [seventy elders]. They will share the burden of the people with you so that you will not have to carry it alone. Tell the people: . . . Now the LORD will give you meat, and you will eat it . . . until it comes out of your nostrils and you loathe it." . . .

But Moses said, ". . . Would they have enough if flocks and herds were slaughtered for them? Would they have enough if all the fish in the sea were caught for them?"

The LORD answered Moses, "Is the LORD's arm too short? Now you will see whether or not what I say will come true for you."

Devotional

The people of Israel are clamoring for meat and blame Moses for their discomfort and limited provision of food. Instead of asking and trusting God for his provision, they demand Moses rescue them from their pain. Moses responds immediately, jumping in to save them. In fact, Moses *overfunctions* by doing for them what they can and should do for themselves.

Overfunctioning is particularly difficult to identify and remedy because we often get rewarded for it, especially in the church. However, it damages friendships, marriages, churches, workplaces, and families. As a result, we become resentful (like Moses); we perpetuate the immaturity of others (like the complaining Israelites); we damage community; and we stray from what God has purposed for us. Perhaps most importantly, we don't have to face the fears that drive our overfunctioning in the first place.[74]

When we overfunction, we end up believing that we are indispensable—that things will fall apart if we let go. Actually, the opposite is true. If we let go of our overfunctioning ways, then God's work will prosper—in us and, ultimately, in those we seek to serve. When Moses does let go and cries out to God, even in his frustration, God intervenes.

Question to Consider

In what areas of life do you sometimes feel indispensable? (For example, at home, at work, at church, in a friendship, with your extended family.) How might God be inviting you to let go?

Prayer

> *Father, help me to trust that you really are on the throne, that your arm is not too short to take care of the people and situations I care so much about. Grant to me a healthy sensitivity to relationships when I am doing for others what they can and should do for themselves. And may I rest in the freedom that comes from being deeply grounded in your love. In Jesus' name, amen.*

Conclude with Silence (2 minutes)

DAY 5 MORNING/MIDDAY OFFICE

Silence and Stillness before God (2 minutes)

Scripture Reading: Luke 4:16–19, 28–30

> [Jesus] went to Nazareth, where he had been brought up, and on the Sabbath day he went into the synagogue, as was his custom. He stood up to read, and the scroll of the

prophet Isaiah was handed to him. Unrolling it, he found
the place where it is written:

> "The Spirit of the Lord is on me,
>   because he has anointed me
>   to proclaim good news to the poor.
> He has sent me to proclaim freedom for the prisoners
>   and recovery of sight for the blind,
> to set the oppressed free,
>   to proclaim the year of the Lord's favor." ...

All the people in the synagogue were furious when they
heard this. They got up, drove him out of the town, and
took him to the brow of the hill on which the town was
built, in order to throw him off the cliff. But he walked
right through the crowd and went on his way.

Devotional

It seems that almost everyone had expectations to impose on
Jesus' life. He disappointed a lot of people, even to the point they
wanted to throw him off a cliff! Yet he was secure in his Father's
love and remained faithful to his God-given identity and purpose.

Although we may not routinely be in danger of being thrown
from a cliff, we too have to sometimes face down the pressures
and expectations other people want to impose on us. One very
helpful way to clarify this challenge is to understand a concept
called *differentiation*. Differentiation refers to a person's capacity

to define his or her own life's goals and values apart from the pressures of those around them. A differentiated person has the ability to think clearly and carefully, to set priorities and make decisions.

Differentiation means you know how to hold on to who you are and who you are not regardless of your circumstances. Your level of differentiation is determined by how well you are able to affirm your values and goals apart from the pressures around you (separateness), while remaining close to people important to you (togetherness). Your convictions, goals, and values don't change, even under pressure. You can make healthy choices, before God, without being controlled by the approval or disapproval of others.

Differentiation is sometimes uncomfortable, but tolerating discomfort is foundational to maturing and growth. The good news is, every small step of differentiation we take is actually a giant step toward making our lives a gift to the world.[75]

Question to Consider

In which of your relationships might God be inviting you to differentiate, to tolerate short-term discomfort for the sake of long-term growth—in you and in those around you?

Prayer

Father, I admit that my fear and anxiety sometimes cause me to say and do things I regret. When my values are being violated or I feel pressured to make a decision I don't want to make, help

*me to speak up or stand my ground. Grant me the courage to
take steps today to differentiate in ways that will lead me, and
others, to greater maturity. In Jesus' name, amen.*

Conclude with Silence (2 minutes)

DAY 5 MIDDAY/EVENING OFFICE

Silence and Stillness before God (2 minutes)

Scripture Reading: John 9:18–23

> They still did not believe that he had been blind and had
> received his sight until they sent for the man's parents. "Is
> this your son?" they asked. "Is this the one you say was born
> blind? How is it that now he can see?"
>
> "We know he is our son," the parents answered, "and
> we know he was born blind. But how he can see now, or
> who opened his eyes, we don't know. Ask him. He is of age;
> he will speak for himself." His parents said this because
> they were afraid of the Jewish leaders, who already had
> decided that anyone who acknowledged that Jesus was the
> Messiah would be put out of the synagogue. That was why
> his parents said, "He is of age; ask him."

Devotional

In contrast to their fearless, truth-telling son, the parents
in this story are afraid of the religious leaders. Why? To be

removed from the synagogue was to become a non-person in first-century Jewish society. Yet we learn an important truth from the blind man's parents: When we are *not* the same person on the inside as we appear to be on the outside, there are painful consequences. Parker Palmer notes a few of those consequences for us:

- We lose touch with our souls and disappear into our roles. . . .
- We sense that something is missing in our lives and search the world for it, not understanding that what is missing is us.
- We feel fraudulent, even invisible, because we are not in the world as we really are.
- Our inauthenticity and projections make real relationships impossible, leading to loneliness.
- Our contributions to the world—especially through the work we do—are tainted by duplicity. . . .

The divided life is a wounded life, and the soul keeps calling us to heal the wound. Ignore that call, and we find ourselves trying to numb our pain with an anesthetic of choice, be it substance abuse, overwork, consumerism, or mindless media noise. Such anesthetics are easy to come by in a society that wants to keep us divided *and* unaware of our pain. . . . But there can be no greater suffering than living a lifelong lie.[76]

The parents of the healed blind man choose *not* to make the changes that following Jesus require. Their fears of being cast out of the synagogue and the negative reaction of the Jewish leaders are too great. They didn't appreciate that Jesus was with them, and that he could give them more than enough grace and power to carry them into a new future.

Question to Consider

Consider your interactions over the last twenty-four hours. In what ways, if any, did you choose your actions or words specifically to either gain approval or to avoid disapproval?

Prayer

> *Lord, grant me grace to be free from the fear of what other people think. Show me where and how I make decisions to get the approval of those around me (or to avoid their disapproval). Free me from a divided life that I might be the same person on the inside that I am on the outside. In Jesus' name, amen.*

Conclude with Silence (2 minutes)

Fight
Cleanly

DAILY OFFICES

Week Seven

No two people are alike. God created each of us different—with unique preferences, desires, values, and dreams. When we don't know how to negotiate these differences with others, we can feel threatened and respond in immature ways, especially when under stress. As disciples of Jesus, we are called to navigate our differences and resolve conflict in God-honoring ways. When we Fight Cleanly, we use an emotionally healthy relationship tool designed to help us resolve conflicts as mature Christ followers.

To implement this skill, however, requires ongoing renewal and transformation, something the Daily Office helps us to do by routinely placing ourselves in God's presence. In the power of the Holy Spirit, we receive the courage to quit blaming others and take responsibility to ask for what we want or need. When we linger in God's presence, he softens us to become more generous. And most importantly, we receive God's love in such a way that we are able to give it away to those around us.

ADDITIONAL RESOURCES

- *The Emotionally Healthy Relationships Workbook*, Session 7
- *The Emotionally Healthy Relationships DVD*, Session 7

DAY 1 MORNING/MIDDAY PRAYER

Silence and Stillness before God (2 minutes)

Scripture Reading: Matthew 10:34–36

> Do not suppose that I have come to bring peace to the earth.
> I did not come to bring peace, but a sword. For I have come
> to turn
>
> > "a man against his father,
> > > a daughter against her mother,
> > a daughter-in-law against her mother-in-law—
> > > a man's enemies will be the members of his own
> > > household."

Devotional

Perhaps one of the most misapplied teachings in the New Testament is Jesus' proclamation: "Blessed are the peacemakers, for they will be called children of God" (Matthew 5:9). Too many people think that what Jesus calls us to in this verse is a kind of blanket passivity and false appeasement to ensure that nobody gets upset.

We forget that conflict and trouble were near constants in the life and mission of Jesus. He disrupted the false peace that everyone around him wanted, including his disciples, the crowds, the religious leaders, the Romans, those buying and selling in

the temple—even his own family. Jesus shows us that healthy
Christians do not avoid legitimate conflict.

When we avoid conflict and appease people out of fear, we are
false peacemakers. Jesus shows us that true peace will never come
by trying to pretend that what's wrong is right. True peacemakers
love God, others, and themselves enough to disrupt false peace
when necessary.

Nonetheless, unresolved conflicts remain one of the greatest
tensions in Christians' lives today. We don't know what to do
with these difficult issues and so we ignore them, hoping against
hope they will somehow go away. They don't. And we all learn,
sooner or later, that we can't build Christ's kingdom on false
peace and pretense. Only the truth will do.[77]

Question to Consider

In what kind of situations, or with whom, are you routinely
tempted to avoid conflict and settle for a false peace?

Prayer

> *Lord, forgive me for pretending that things are okay when
> they're not. I often ignore difficult issues and problems because I
> want to avoid conflict and messiness. Help me, I pray, to follow
> the way of Jesus, to be a true peacemaker in all my relationships,
> so that the kingdom of God might be as evident in my life as it
> is in heaven. In Jesus' name, amen.*

Conclude with Silence (2 minutes)

DAY 1 MIDDAY/EVENING PRAYER

Silence and Stillness before God (2 minutes)

Scripture Reading: Isaiah 58:9–11

> If you do away with the yoke of oppression,
>   with the pointing finger and malicious talk,
> and if you spend yourselves in behalf of the hungry
>   and satisfy the needs of the oppressed,
> then your light will rise in the darkness,
>   and your night will become like the noonday.
> The LORD will guide you always;
>   he will satisfy your needs in a sun-scorched land
>   and will strengthen your frame.
> You will be like a well-watered garden,
>   like a spring whose waters never fail.

Devotional

During Isaiah's time (about 700 BC), God's people were devout—they prayed, fasted, and memorized Scripture. However, they also had a problem with "the pointing finger and malicious talk." Their relationships were marked by impatience, a judgmental spirit, and irritation. Perhaps their disconnected spirituality sounded like this: *I can't stand you, but at least I prayed and read Scripture this morning!* They failed to see that it is impossible to think about the spiritual life apart from loving our neighbors.

Jesus' teaching on love is radical. He goes so far as to say that the degree to which we love our "enemies"—those who hurt us, irritate us, drive us crazy—is the true indicator of our spiritual maturity. Another way to think of this is that our enemies are our "saint-makers," the means God uses to deeply and powerfully transform us. In this sense, enemies are not interruptions or obstacles but gifts-in-disguise from God.

Jesus repeatedly taught that loving God and loving others are inseparable. Why? He knew how easy it is to compartmentalize our thoughts and beliefs from our actions, that we could pray and even practice spiritual disciplines and still fail to love the people with whom we live.

Question to Consider

If it's true that our enemies can be gifts-in-disguise from God, who in your life might be a "saint-maker"? In what way(s) might God be using this person to transform you?

Prayer

Lord, fill me with your love today for my saint-maker, _____. Help me to see this person not as an enemy but as a gift-in-disguise, the means by which you are helping me to become more like Jesus. I open the door of my heart for you and ask that you would help me to see my saint-maker through your eyes, and to love them as you do. In Jesus' name, amen.

Conclude with Silence (2 minutes)

DAY 2 MORNING/MIDDAY PRAYER

Silence and Stillness before God (2 minutes)

Scripture Reading: Psalm 56:1–4, 8

> Be merciful to me, my God,
>> for my enemies are in hot pursuit;
>> all day long they press their attack.
> My adversaries pursue me all day long;
>> in their pride many are attacking me.
> When I am afraid, I put my trust in you.
>> In God, whose word I praise—
> in God I trust and am not afraid.
>> What can mere mortals do to me? . . .
> Record my misery;
>> list my tears on your scroll—
>> are they not in your record?

Devotional

Conflicts are stressful and painful. At worst, they can even be violent and destructive. Yet they also have the potential to lead us into intense and powerful spiritual encounters. They are more than a disruption in our otherwise peaceful life. Why? Because they lead us into uncertainty, a loss of control, and a deep sense of disorientation. And that can be good!

The pages of Scripture describe David as a man after God's own heart. What few realize, however, is how closely this characteristic is connected to the way he handled loss, disappointments, and conflicts, even when his very life was threatened. David often spoke and sang about his hardships and difficult relationships. For him, they were vehicles of God's revelation.

We observe this in the book of Psalms—which includes many prayers and hymns written by David—and remains one of the most beloved books of the Bible. More than half of the 150 psalms are laments that give voice to the hard, difficult aspects of life. Scholar Walter Brueggemann has rightly noted that pain and suffering is the center of the three-part pattern we see in Psalms:

- *Orientation*, in which life makes sense and we enjoy God.
- *Disorientation*, in which we are hurt, suffering, and wondering where God is.
- *New orientation*, in which God breaks in and we meet him in a new way.[78]

God assures us of his love and passion for us. He is committed to bringing each of us into a *new orientation*—a new place with him—so that he can do a new thing in us and for us. But in order to get there, we have to be willing to go through *disorientation*.

Question to Ponder

When was the last time God led you into a season of disorientation that ultimately resulted in a new orientation with fresh insights and growth?

Prayer

*Lord, I am much more likely to try to avoid pain and conflict
than walk into it. Grant me the grace and trust I need to wait
on you, especially through hard times, sorrows, and relational
stress. Help me to stay with you through my disorientation
so that I might receive the new things you want to do in and
through me. In Jesus' name, amen.*

Conclude with Silence (2 minutes)

DAY 2 MIDDAY/EVENING PRAYER

Silence and Stillness before God (2 minutes)

Scripture Reading: John 21:18–19

"Very truly I tell you, when you were younger you dressed
yourself and went where you wanted; but when you are
old you will stretch out your hands, and someone else
will dress you and lead you where you do not want to
go." Jesus said this to indicate the kind of death by
which Peter would glorify God. Then he said to him,
"Follow me!"

Devotional

Jesus had a different vision of spiritual maturity: It is the ability
and willingness to be led where you would rather not go. It is
recognizing that it is foolish to try to remain in control of life.

Instead, he offers to Peter, and to us, the truth that following him sometimes requires being led to unknown and difficult places, some of which involve conflicts with others. Author David Benner says it well:

> The way of ascent is the way of control, willfulness, grasping, and clutching. The way of descent is the way of surrender, willingness, and letting go. Nothing that we fail to give away will ever really be ours. Only that which has died can be raised from the dead. Christian spirituality is a path of descent, not ascent. . . .
>
> Rather than being a spirituality of self-improvement . . . it is a spirituality of following Jesus on a journey of dying to our false self so that we might discover our true and larger identity in Christ. . . .
>
> Life brings us a steady flow of opportunities to practice choosing surrender. Events that we would never choose enter our life quite regularly—sometimes as small interruptions to our plans for the day, and other times as crises that change our life forever. Regardless of their magnitude, these events serve as reminders that, despite our efforts and desires, we are not in control.[79]

The great news, however, is that as we discover Jesus' downward way of surrender and letting go, we also discover the richness and beauty in life that God intends.

Question to Consider

In the last few days, what "small interruptions" have come into your life that offer an opportunity to practice choosing surrender?

Prayer

Abba, Father, you are good, and your love endures forever. I open my hands in surrender to you. Expose any unhealthy attachments in me and help me to trust you in all things. Help me to let go of the illusion that I need control, approval, or earthly security for my happiness. In Jesus' name, amen.

Conclude with Silence (2 minutes)

DAY 3 MORNING/MIDDAY PRAYER

Silence and Stillness before God (2 minutes)

Scripture Reading: Genesis 32:22–31

That night Jacob got up and took his two wives, his two female servants and his eleven sons and crossed the ford of the Jabbok. After he had sent them across the stream, he sent over all his possessions. So Jacob was left alone, and a man wrestled with him till daybreak. When the man saw that he could not overpower him, he touched the socket of Jacob's hip so that his hip was wrenched as he wrestled with the man. Then the man said, "Let me go, for it is daybreak."

But Jacob replied, "I will not let you go unless you bless me."

The man asked him, "What is your name?"

"Jacob," he answered.

Then the man said, "Your name will no longer be Jacob, but Israel, because you have struggled with God and with humans and have overcome."

Jacob said, "Please tell me your name."

But he replied, "Why do you ask my name?" Then he blessed him there.

So Jacob called the place Peniel, saying, "It is because I saw God face to face, and yet my life was spared."

The sun rose above him as he passed Peniel, and he was limping because of his hip.

Devotional

When Jacob was a young man, he used trickery and deceit to steal the birthright and blessing that rightfully belonged to his older brother, Esau. As a result, he had to flee from his brother's murderous wrath. After twenty-five years had passed—years in which there was no contact between them—Jacob begins a journey back home. He will face the conflict head on and reconcile with Esau if he can. God had said to him, "I will be with you" (Genesis 31:3).

In the midst of his uncertainty about what might happen, a man (believed by some to be the pre-incarnate Christ) wrestled with Jacob in the night and struck his hip out of joint. Not long after, Jacob and Esau met and were reconciled. Here is how author John Paul Lederach describes what we can learn from these ancient brothers about God's presence in our conflicts:

> The call [Jacob] received [was] to turn toward all that he feared and walk back to his brother, not knowing what would happen. And the promise of God was not that all would be fine, or that all would be taken care of well ahead of his arrival. The promise was a simple "I will be *with* you." …
>
> Ultimately, reconciliation is a journey toward and through conflict. In this instance, God does not promise to do the work for Jacob. God does not promise that he will take care of everything and level the road for Jacob. God promises to accompany him, to be present. …
>
> We will find God present throughout the journey toward reconciliation in the depths of fear, in the hopelessness of the dark nights, in the tears of reconnection. … The pathway through conflict toward reconciliation is filled with God-encounters, if we have the eyes to see, and the heart to feel. …
>
> Conflict opens a path, a holy path, toward revelation and reconciliation.[80]

Conflicts offer us revelation and the possibility of reconciliation, but they can also leave us limping—if we allow God to do that work in us. They become opportunities God can use to break our pride and teach us to depend on him more fully.

Question to Consider

In what ways does God's simple promise, "I will be *with* you," give you courage to move toward your fears and toward reconciliation with someone with whom you have a conflict?

Prayer

Lord, I long for the courage of Jacob—to move toward rather than away from those with whom I have conflict. The uncertainty scares me. But I also believe and claim the promise that you will be with me. I ask that this journey of reconciliation will become a path of revelation—a place in which I encounter you in a new way. In Jesus' name, amen.

Conclude with Silence (2 minutes)

DAY 3 MIDDAY/EVENING PRAYER

Silence and Stillness before God (2 minutes)

Scripture Reading: Matthew 5:43–48

You have heard that it was said, "Love your neighbor and hate your enemy." But I tell you, love your enemies and pray for those who persecute you, that you may be children of your Father in heaven. He causes his sun to rise on the evil and the good, and sends rain on the righteous and the unrighteous. If you love those who love you, what reward will you get? Are not even the tax collectors doing that?

And if you greet only your own people, what are you doing more than others? Do not even pagans do that? Be perfect, therefore, as your heavenly Father is perfect.

Devotional

Let's face it. It is hard, if not impossible, to love unconditionally—especially when it comes to our enemies. That is why we are to pray. A miracle is required for this to happen, but God is good at miracles. It's no accident that Jesus begins his Sermon on the Mount (Matthew 5–7) with, "Blessed are the poor in spirit" (Matthew 5:3a). Only those who are know they are completely helpless without God's supernatural help can love this way.

Margaret Guenther, a well-known writer on the spiritual life, offers this application for loving our enemies:

[Jesus'] standard of forgiveness is radical, breathtaking, seemingly impossible. I'm not sure I'm up for the challenge. But at least I can try.

In the meantime, it's a good idea to think about enemies from time to time.... Who might see me as the enemy? To this question, I usually answer, "Me? Who could possibly see me, hard-working and generally well-meaning *me* as an enemy?" It can be a painful exercise in self-examination to reflect on whom we might have hurt, diminished, or dismissed, intentionally or carelessly. And then to ponder: what am I going to do about it? And who are my enemies? What can I learn from them? Justly or unjustly, those who wish us harm can teach us a great deal about ourselves. Am I being condescending when I think that I am gracious? Speaking harshly and hurtfully when I think I am helpfully direct? Coldhearted when I ignore the need of a brother or sister? Arrogant when I assume that my way . . . is the best and only way? If we pay attention and are willing to look at ourselves honestly, our enemies can teach us a lot.[81]

The question, of course, is do we really want to learn that much? Do we want to learn from those whom we've hurt? The answer is both yes and no. But if we pray for the miraculous courage and humility to do so, "we can be sure that our enemies can teach us a lot."

Question to Consider

Who is someone that you suspect you may "have hurt, diminished, or dismissed, intentionally or carelessly"? What might God's invitation be when you consider the question, "What am I going to do about it?"

Prayer

Lord, wrestling with this question about how I may have hurt someone else is difficult and painful. I can easily identify how people have hurt me and treated me poorly. But to learn from those who think I am the enemy? That is so much harder. By your Holy Spirit, grant me the grace to see the flaws in my

*character and to take any steps you might have for me this day.
In Jesus' name, amen.*

Conclude with Silence (2 minutes)

DAY 4 MORNING/MIDDAY OFFICE

Silence and Stillness before God (2 minutes)

Scripture Reading: Matthew 5:1–7

Now when Jesus saw the crowds, he went up on a mountainside and sat down. His disciples came to him, and he began to teach them.

He said:

"Blessed are the poor in spirit,
for theirs is the kingdom of heaven.
Blessed are those who mourn,
for they will be comforted.
Blessed are the meek,
for they will inherit the earth.
Blessed are those who hunger and thirst for
righteousness,
for they will be filled.
Blessed are the merciful,
for they will be shown mercy."

Devotional

Dorothy Day (1897–1980) was a cofounder of the Catholic Worker Movement. Best known for her radical embodiment of the gospel through feeding the hungry and housing the homeless, she also engaged in a radical pacifism as a witness to loving all people. Her life and writings continue to serve as a sign to the world of the mercy of God in a harsh world. This story gives us a glimpse into her deep insight into Jesus and his kingdom:

> It was ... almost thirty-five years ago that I first met Dorothy Day. She was sitting at a table, talking with a woman who was, I quickly realized, quite drunk, yet determined to carry on a conversation.... The woman ... had a large purple-red birthmark along the right side of her forehead. She kept touching it as she uttered one exclamatory remark after another, none of which seemed to get the slightest rise from the person sitting opposite her.
>
> I found myself increasingly confused by what seemed to be an interminable, essentially absurd exchange taking place between the two middle-aged women. When would it end—the alcoholic ranting and the silent nodding, occasionally interrupted by a brief question, which only served, maddeningly, to wind up the already overtalkative one rather than wind her down? Finally silence fell upon the room. Dorothy Day asked the woman if she would mind an interruption. She got up

and came over to me. She said, "Are you waiting to talk with one of us?"

One of us: with those three words she had cut through layers of self-importance, a lifetime of bourgeois privilege, and scraped the hard bone of pride: "Vanity of vanities; all is vanity." With those three words, so quietly and politely spoken, she had indirectly told me what the Catholic Worker Movement is all about and what she herself was like.[82]

Dorothy Day understood that a genuine relationship with Jesus results in a mercy that makes us softer toward others, not a morality that makes us both harder and superior.

Jesus turned the values of the world upside down. His kingdom, he announces, belongs to the "poor in spirit," those on the bottom, those who feel crushed, and are completely dependent on others. He makes clear it is not the aggressively self-seeking or the overachievers who will inherit the earth, but the powerless, the sad, the meek, those whom the world considers failures. Those on the top will be on the bottom, and those on the bottom will be on the top.

As we grow in grace to see people as Jesus did, we discover that our defenses diminish and our hearts become softer, especially when we are in tension or conflict with those around us.

Question to Consider

Jesus said, "I desire mercy, not sacrifice" (Matthew 9:13). What is one concrete way you can show mercy to someone today?

Prayer

A PRAYER OF ST. FURSEY

(Seventh century, Ireland)

The arms of God be around my shoulders,
the touch of the Holy Spirit upon my head,
the sign of Christ's cross upon my forehead,
the sound of the Holy Spirit in my ears,
the fragrance of the Holy Spirit in my nostrils,
the vision of heaven's company in my eyes,
the conversation of heaven's company on my lips,
the work of God's church with my hands,
the service of God and my neighbor in my feet,
a home for God in my heart,
and to God, the father of all, my entire being.
Amen.

Conclude with Silence (2 minutes)

DAY 4 MIDDAY/EVENING OFFICE

Silence and Stillness before God (2 minutes)

Scripture Reading: Luke 18:9–14

To some who were confident of their own righteousness
and looked down on everyone else, Jesus told this parable:
"Two men went up to the temple to pray, one a Pharisee

and the other a tax collector. The Pharisee stood by himself and prayed: 'God, I thank you that I am not like other people—robbers, evildoers, adulterers—or even like this tax collector. I fast twice a week and give a tenth of all I get.'

"But the tax collector stood at a distance. He would not even look up to heaven, but beat his breast and said, 'God, have mercy on me, a sinner.'

"I tell you that this man, rather than the other, went home justified before God. For all those who exalt themselves will be humbled, and those who humble themselves will be exalted."

Devotional

One of my favorite sayings comes from a story in *The Desert Fathers* about a fourth-century monk named John the Short. A jealous fellow monk once approached John as he was teaching at the front of the church.

[The monk] said, "John, your cup is full of poison."

John answered, "Yes . . . it is. But you said that when you could only see the outside; I wonder what you would say if you saw the inside."[83]

John the Short is not defensive in his response. He does not attack the monk or fire off a joke to deflect the conversation away from himself. He courageously admits his vulnerability and what he knows to be true about himself. Like the apostle Paul, he affirms, "I [am] the worst of sinners" (1 Timothy 1:16). John the Short didn't retreat into a self-protective shell and stop serving others. Rather, he remained open and vulnerable to the one who criticized him.

If our desire is to lead and serve others, we have to come to grips with this plain, hard fact: the degree to which we ignore sinful, ugly parts of ourselves is the degree to which our ability to love and lead others is limited and impaired.[84]

Question to Consider

What might it look like for you to respond to criticism in the nondefensive, humble way John the Short did?

Prayer

Father, when I feel attacked, all I want to do is defend myself and attack back. I ask that you fill me with a profound sense of your love today. And do a work in me to change my defensiveness to humility, that your tenderness and love might flow through me. In Jesus' name, amen.

Conclude with Silence (2 minutes)

DAY 5 MORNING/MIDDAY PRAYER

Silence and Stillness before God (2 minutes)

Scripture Reading: John 18:2–4, 10–11

> Now Judas, who betrayed him, knew the place, because
> Jesus had often met there with his disciples. So Judas came
> to the garden, guiding a detachment of soldiers and some
> officials from the chief priests and the Pharisees. They were
> carrying torches, lanterns and weapons.
>
> Jesus, knowing all that was going to happen to him,
> went out and asked them, "Who is it you want?" . . .
>
> Then Simon Peter, who had a sword, drew it and struck
> the high priest's servant, cutting off his right ear. (The
> servant's name was Malchus.)
>
> Jesus commanded Peter, "Put your sword away! Shall I
> not drink the cup the Father has given me?"

Devotional

It's not hard to relate to Peter's anger at the injustice of Jesus'
arrest. In his outrage, he lashes out in physical violence. Imagine
the scene, the blood, the chaos. And he did it *for* Jesus. However,
he simultaneously failed to listen *to* the voice of Jesus and is
rebuked by him. He thought he was proving his love, defend-
ing Jesus with an act of bravery, but in the process, he violated
the very nature of the love Jesus lived and died for. When we
don't pay attention to what Jesus is doing and saying—when we
misunderstand what love requires—relational breakdowns and
chaos inevitably follow.

Author Henri Nouwen articulated the struggle many of us
have when it comes to loving others. He described two voices

within. One voice constantly pushed him to succeed and achieve. It was this voice Nouwen says he spent most of his life heeding. Following this voice led him to teach at such prestigious universities as Notre Dame, Harvard, and Yale. It pressed him to write more than a book a year. But the constant demands that heeding this voice placed on his speaking schedule and ministry threatened to suffocate his spiritual life. He was praying poorly and living isolated from people.

The other voice within was God's voice. This voice reassured him he was unconditionally loved. He had nothing to prove. This voice told him the goal of ministry was to recognize the Lord's voice, his face, and his touch in every person he met.

Only in the last ten years of his life, Nouwen said, did he truly listen to that second voice. The transition occurred when he resigned his professorship at Harvard to accept a position as pastor of a L'Arche Community of mentally handicapped people near Toronto, Ontario, Canada. And it was from these men and women that he learned about love and community.[85]

With the multiple demands and constant pressure of our lives, it can be difficult to pay attention to God's voice. When we don't, we easily go the way of Peter and pull out our swords when people appear to threaten what we love or the way we think things should be. Jesus, on the other hand, offers us another model—a love demonstrated through submission to the Father and humility in our relationships.

Question to Consider

In what situation, and with whom, are you tempted to "cut off someone's ear," to defend yourself, or something you love, by acting in ways that are not truly loving?

Prayer

> *Father, I relate to Peter more than I care to admit. Forgive me for my impatience and self-will that wants always to be in charge of myself and others. I so often fail to recognize your voice in the people I encounter. Deliver me from the external and internal forces that keep me from listening to your voice of love and from loving the people around me. In Jesus' name, amen.*

Conclude with Silence (2 minutes)

DAY 5 MIDDAY/EVENING PRAYER

Silence and Stillness before God (2 minutes)

Scripture Reading: Ephesians 4:30–32

> And do not grieve the Holy Spirit of God, with whom you were sealed for the day of redemption. Get rid of all bitterness, rage and anger, brawling and slander, along with every form of malice. Be kind and compassionate to one another, forgiving each other, just as in Christ God forgave you.

Devotional

We want to obey Scripture's command to get rid of all bitterness and be forgiving to one another. The question is, how?

A number of years ago, William Meninger, a Trappist monk who has dedicated his life to prayer for over fifty years, visited our church in New York City to teach us some of what he's learned. One of the things he shared was a "Compassion Meditation Prayer," the purpose of which was to help us forgive and let go of bitterness.

An adapted and shortened version of the prayer is included below. It is meant to be prayed for someone you might consider an enemy or someone with whom you are in a conflict. It may even be someone from your past, living or dead, for whom forgiveness is still possible and overdue.

> May you be happy, may you be free.
> May you be loving, may you be loved.
> May you know the fulfillment of what
>   God has planned for you.
> May you experience God's deep, profound love for you.
> May Jesus Christ be formed in you.
> May you know his peace that passes all understanding.
> May all good things be yours.
> May Jesus' joy be in you and may that joy be complete.
> May you know the Lord in all his goodness and compassion.
> May you be protected from the evil one amidst every
>   temptation that comes your way.

May the Holy Spirit fill and permeate your entire being.
May you see his glory
May you be forgiven of every sin.
I forgive you (or "will try to forgive you") of every wound
   and hurt with all my heart.
May God's goodness and mercy follow you all the days
   of your life.[86]

Praying this for a person who has wounded us is no small task, but it is a significant step forward. Let me invite you to pray it repeatedly, even if you don't feel it. You can trust God will heal your wounds over time and do a work in you, by the Holy Spirit, that you cannot do in yourself.

QUESTION TO CONSIDER

As you consider a person who has hurt you, what words or phrases from the Compassion Prayer impact you most?

Prayer

Jesus, thank you for loving me with the kind of loving compassion expressed in this prayer. I long to be the kind of person who sincerely feels and prays like this—especially for those who hurt me. But I am a long way from that now. I ask that you do a profound work in me so that I might truly love like you. In your name I pray, amen.

Conclude with Silence (2 minutes)

Develop a
"Rule of Life" to
Implement Emotionally
Healthy Skills

Jesus forcefully taught the key to being his disciple is to not simply hear his words but to put them into practice (Matthew 7:24–27). This is nowhere more important than in implementing the two great commandments of loving God and loving our neighbor. This isn't something we can leave to chance. We need a thoughtful and intentional plan.

A Rule of Life is not a *rule* in the same sense that word is commonly used today. The root of the word traces back to the ancient Greek word for *trellis*. It referred to a structure, such as those designed to help grapevines grow upward, becoming more fruitful and productive. A Rule of Life has a similar function and objective. It is a support structure that helps us to grow in Christ. It is an intentional plan centered around spiritual practices that enable us to pay attention to God and keep him in the center of all our relationships.

ADDITIONAL RESOURCES

- *The Emotionally Healthy Relationships Workbook*, Session 8
- *The Emotionally Healthy Relationships DVD*, Session 8

DAY 1 MORNING/MIDDAY PRAYER

Silence and Stillness before God (2 minutes)

Scripture Reading: 1 John 4:19–21

> We love because he first loved us. Whoever claims to love
> God yet hates a brother or sister is a liar. For whoever does
> not love their brother and sister, whom they have seen,
> cannot love God, whom they have not seen. And he has
> given us this command: Anyone who loves God must also
> love their brother and sister.

Devotional

Few truths in Scripture force us to take as deep and hard a look
inside our hearts as does this passage from 1 John: *There is no
possibility of loving God without loving one another.* In his novel
The Brothers Karamazov, Fyodor Dostoevsky captures the
necessity of making difficult, intentional choices if we are to
obey this command.

He tells the story of a wealthy woman who asks an elderly
monk how she can know if God exists. He tells her no explanation or argument can achieve this, only the practice of "active
love." The monk speaks glowingly of love for God, which comes
as a result of love for others.

The wealthy woman then confesses that she sometimes
dreams about a life of loving service to others. At such times she
thinks perhaps she will become a Sister of Mercy, live in holy

poverty, and serve the poor in the humblest way. But then it crosses her mind how ungrateful some of the people she would serve are likely to be. They would probably complain that the soup she served wasn't hot enough or that the bread wasn't fresh enough or the bed was too hard. She confesses that she couldn't bear such ingratitude—and so her dreams about serving others vanish, and once again she finds herself wondering if there is a God.

To this the wise monk responds, "Love in practice is a harsh and dreadful thing compared with love in dreams." [87]

Loving well is the goal of the Christian life. And as the wise monk knew, this is easier in our dreams than in practice. It requires that we grow into spiritual and emotional adulthood in Christ, the rewards of which are rich beyond measure.

Question to Consider

Briefly reflect on your relationships with a few people you routinely interact with. What "harsh and dreadful things" might love require of you in these relationships?

Prayer

> *Lord, I relate to the perspective of the wealthy woman more than I care to admit. Grant me the grace of patience to persevere in loving others, even when it requires "harsh and dreadful things" of me. May your love so fill me that loving in practice becomes my instinctive and natural response. In Jesus' name, amen.*

Conclude with Silence (2 minutes)

DAY 1 MIDDAY/EVENING PRAYER

Silence and Stillness before God (2 minutes)

Scripture Reading: Numbers 20:7–12

> The LORD said to Moses, "Take the staff, and you and your
> brother Aaron gather the assembly together. Speak to that
> rock before their eyes and it will pour out its water. You will
> bring water out of the rock for the community so they and
> their livestock can drink."
>
> So Moses took the staff from the LORD's presence,
> just as he commanded him. He and Aaron gathered the
> assembly together in front of the rock and Moses said to
> them, "Listen, you rebels, must we bring you water out of
> this rock?" Then Moses raised his arm and struck the rock
> twice with his staff. Water gushed out, and the community
> and their livestock drank.
>
> But the LORD said to Moses and Aaron, "Because you
> did not trust in me enough to honor me as holy in the sight
> of the Israelites, you will not bring this community into the
> land I give them."

Devotional

Moses worked and waited for almost forty years to enter the
Promised Land. Having started with 603,550 men—not to men-
tion all the women and children—his patience was repeatedly
tested to the limit by a seemingly endless barrage of complaints

and disputes. When the people cry about their lack of food and water and accuse Moses of bringing them out into the desert to die, Moses is furious.

At this point, he is also exhausted and has little capacity to manage his anger and resentment. So he lashes out and rebukes the people, calling them "rebels." Rather than honoring and obeying God, he relies on an old strategy of striking the rock because, hey, why not, it worked once before (Exodus 17:6).

In his frustration with the people, Moses willfully disregards God's instruction to speak to the rock and instead strikes it twice. One scholar suggests that, in striking the rock, Moses was actually striking out at God:

> There was an element of sacrilege in striking the rock, for it symbolized God. God is often likened to a rock (e.g., Psalm 18:2; 31:3; 42:9). Paul, [in writing about the wilderness years], says, '[They] drank from the supernatural Rock which followed them, and the Rock was Christ' (1 Corinthians 10:4)."[88]

Question to Consider

Moses commits an act of rebellion when he disregards God's instructions. He still does God's work, but from a place of frustration and on his own terms. In what ways, if any, do you recognize this pattern in your own life?

Prayer

> *Father, sometimes when things don't go according to my plan,*
> *I respond a lot like Moses by taking out my frustrations on*
> *others or taking matters into my own hands. Help me to slow*
> *down and look to you. Fill me with the power of the Holy*
> *Spirit so that in difficult moments I can still do your will and*
> *treat others with tenderness, patience, and kindness. In Jesus'*
> *name, amen.*

Conclude with Silence (2 minutes)

DAY 2 MORNING/MIDDAY PRAYER

Silence and Stillness before God (2 minutes)

Scripture Reading: Matthew 26:26–28

> While they were eating, Jesus took bread, and when he had
> given thanks, he broke it and gave it to his disciples, saying,
> "Take and eat; this is my body."
>
> Then he took a cup, and when he had given thanks, he
> gave it to them, saying, "Drink from it, all of you. This is
> my blood of the covenant, which is poured out for many
> for the forgiveness of sins."

Devotional

At his final meal with the disciples, Jesus broke bread as a symbol
of how he was making himself bread, sacrificing his very life for

love. Henri Nouwen summarizes the process of how we too can love—and become bread for the world—by expounding on the four things Jesus did when he broke bread. The bread was *taken*, *blessed*, *broken*, and *given*:

> I must tell you that these four words have become the most important words of my life.... The first step in the spiritual life is to acknowledge with our whole being that we already have been *taken*, or chosen.... When I write you that, I mean that we have been seen by God from all eternity and seen as unique, special, precious beings....
>
> [Then] as the beloved children of God, we are *blessed*. For me personally, prayer becomes more and more a way to listen to the blessing....
>
> *Broken*. The way I am broken tells you something about me. The way you are broken tells me something about you. Our brokenness is as unique as our chosenness and our blessedness....
>
> We are chosen, blessed, and broken so as to be *given*. In the giving it becomes clear that we are chosen, blessed and broken not simply for our own sakes, but so that all we live finds its final significance in its being lived for others.[89] (emphasis added)

Jesus *took*, *blessed*, *broke*, and *gave* the bread of his life to the disciples, and the world. In the same way, he invites us to become bread so we too can love those around us.

Question to Consider

How do you respond to the truth that your life is *taken*, *blessed*, *broken*, and *given*? Which of these four words speaks most to you today?

Prayer

> *Father, I don't mind being blessed, but it isn't always easy for me to allow myself to be taken, broken, and given. But I do want to grow in love, and I offer myself to you that I may be given, by you, as a gift to others this day. In Jesus' name, amen.*

Conclude with Silence (2 minutes)

DAY 2 MIDDAY/EVENING PRAYER

Silence and Stillness before God (2 minutes)

Scripture Reading: Mark 7:1–2, 14–15, 20–23

> The Pharisees and some of the teachers of the law who had come from Jerusalem gathered around Jesus and saw some of his disciples eating food with hands that were defiled, that is, unwashed. . . .
>
> Again Jesus called the crowd to him and said, "Listen to me, everyone, and understand this. Nothing outside a person can defile them by going into them. Rather, it is what comes out of a person that defiles them." . . .
>
> He went on: "What comes out of a person is what defiles

them. For it is from within, out of a person's heart, that evil thoughts come—sexual immorality, theft, murder, adultery, greed, malice, deceit, lewdness, envy, slander, arrogance and folly. All these evils come from inside and defile a person."

Devotional

The religious leaders in Jesus' day were deeply concerned with external indicators of holiness, such as observing strict rules about everything from eating food with properly washed hands to proper observance of Sabbath. Jesus, in contrast, was deeply concerned about internal indicators of holiness, specifically the human heart. He knew that resolutions of "I shall be good" were not enough. We each need the direct intervention of God to give us a new heart, a new nature, and a new Spirit. But conversion is not a onetime spiritual event. God intends that every day be a fresh beginning in which we humbly invite the wind of the Holy Spirit to form us more deeply into people who love him and others like he does.

C. S. Lewis captures this need for ongoing transformation in his story of Eustace, a young boy, who becomes a big, ugly dragon as a consequence of being selfish, stubborn, and unbelieving. After indulging his dragon self to the full, he is hurting and wants nothing more than to go back to being a young boy again. But he can't do it himself.

Eventually, the great lion Aslan (representing Jesus) appears to him and leads him to a beautiful well to bathe. But since he is a dragon, he can't enter the well. When Aslan tells him to undress, Eustace peels off a layer of dragon skin by himself, dropping it to the ground. He feels better, but as he moves toward the pool, he realizes there is yet another hard, rough, scaly layer still on him. Frustrated, in pain, and longing to step into that beautiful bath, he asks himself, "How many skins do I have to take off?"

After three layers, Eustace despairs and gives up. Aslan then says, "You will have to let me undress you." Here is how Eustace later describes to his companions what happened next:

> I was afraid of his claws, I can tell you, but I was pretty nearly desperate now. So I just lay flat down on my back and let him do it.
>
> The very first tear he made was so deep that I thought it had gone right into my heart. And when he began pulling the skin off, it hurt worse than anything I've ever felt. . . .
>
> Well, he peeled the beastly stuff right off—just as I thought I'd done it myself the other three times, only they hadn't hurt—and there it was lying on the grass: only ever so much thicker, and darker, and more knobbly-looking than the others had been. And there was I as smooth and soft as a peeled switch and smaller than I had been. Then he caught hold of me . . . and threw me into the water. It smarted like anything but only for a moment. After that it became perfectly delicious and as soon as I started swimming and splashing I found that all the pain had gone from my arm. And then I saw why. I'd turned into a boy again. . . .
>
> After a bit the lion took me out and dressed me [with his paws] . . . in new clothes.[90]

Gritty self-effort can only take us so far in the transformation process. We each carry deep defects of character that will be changed only when we surrender to God's divine surgery.

Question to Consider

What unhealthy pattern or "dragon skin" do you most desire for God to free you from right now?

Prayer

> *Lord, there are unhealthy relational patterns and character defects hidden deep within me. I know I cannot change myself; that is your work. But I know I have to want it and to surrender myself to it. I open the door of my heart to you, inviting you to remove all that hinders me from being a soft, approachable, and loving person. In Jesus' name, amen.*

Conclude with Silence (2 minutes)

DAY 3 MORNING/MIDDAY PRAYER

Silence and Stillness before God (2 minutes)

Scripture Reading: Colossians 3:22–25

> Slaves, obey your earthly masters in everything; and do it, not only when their eye is on you and to curry their favor, but with sincerity of heart and reverence for the Lord. Whatever you do, work at it with all your heart, as

working for the Lord, not for human masters, since you
know that you will receive an inheritance from the Lord
as a reward. It is the Lord Christ you are serving. Anyone
who does wrong will be repaid for their wrongs, and there
is no favoritism.

Devotional

Throughout history, one's calling has often been narrowly
defined as an occupation (career), a status in life (single or mar-
ried), or as secular or consecrated (lay persons or professional
Christian ministers). As a result, we often think: "Whatever my
calling was, I think I may have missed it." Or, "I'm not trained.
I'm just a regular person." Or, "I'm just working, waiting for my
true calling to reveal itself."

Scripture teaches, however, that every Christian is called by
God at conversion. And that calling encompasses the whole of
our lives. Recovering this truth revolutionizes how we understand our role—in the workplace and in the world—as men and
women sent by Jesus to embody his love.

In the Roman Empire, slaves were property and occupied the
lowest rung on the social hierarchy—which meant the worst and
most demeaning tasks fell to them. Yet the apostle Paul offers
a revolutionary new perspective on their status and role. He
reminds them that it is Christ whom they serve, no matter how
lowly the task. And so they are commissioned by God to model
the love of Jesus in their daily work.

The same principle applies to us. It is Christ whom we

serve. And all of us have the ability to creatively and proactively build emotionally healthy relationships and community in his name—as teachers, janitors, health care workers, lawyers, salespeople, managers, volunteers, cooks, small business owners, actors, students, and administrators.

Wherever we work, regardless of who signs our paycheck (or if we even get a paycheck), we are Christ followers first, called to join with him in restoring the world to what God originally intended it to be.

Question to Consider

What is one small way you can take initiative today to serve Christ by loving those around you?

Prayer

> *Lord, help me believe that you have chosen me and sent me to the world. I need courage to proactively and consistently model the love of Jesus in my relationships. Grant me opportunities to embody and reflect your love to everyone I meet this day. In Jesus' name, amen.*

Conclude with Silence (2 minutes)

DAY 3 MIDDAY/EVENING PRAYER

Silence and Stillness before God (2 minutes)

Scripture Reading: Lamentations 3:21–27a

> Yet this I call to mind
>> and therefore I have hope:
> Because of the LORD's great love we are not
>   consumed,
>> for his compassions never fail.
> They are new every morning;
>> great is your faithfulness.
> I say to myself, "The LORD is my portion;
>> therefore I will wait for him."
> The LORD is good to those whose hope is in him,
>> to the one who seeks him;
> it is good to wait quietly
>> for the salvation of the LORD.

Devotional

The key to loving people, especially in difficult times, requires a deep revelation and experience of the love of God in our own lives. Jeremiah, the author of Lamentations, knew this; so must we. One of the most powerful writers in church history to expound on this love of God was a once obscure woman named Julian.

Julian of Norwich (1342–1416) lived in England during a time of enormous political, social, and economic upheaval. She saw the beginning of the Hundred Years War between England and France. She lived through the bubonic plague, which killed more than a third of Europe's population. And she saw a church divided and in moral compromise with government rulers.

Julian chose to live as an anchoress, withdrawing from society to live in a small room attached to a church in the heart of Norwich. Once she entered her cell, she never returned to the outside world. While the physical realities of her living quarters were painfully cramped, the inner realities of her soul were expansive and filled with transcendent experiences with God.

At about the age of thirty, Julian received sixteen "showings" or visions of God's love, which she meditated on for twenty years before writing of them in her book, *The Revelations of Divine Love*. God showed her that his love and his divine will are at work in all things. She wrote:

> All will be well, and all will be well, and every kind of thing will be well. . . .
>
> I saw hidden in God an exalted and wonderful mystery, which he will make plain and we shall know in heaven. In this knowledge we shall truly see the cause why he allowed sin to come, and in this sight we shall rejoice forever. . . .
>
> Another understanding is this: that there are many deeds so evilly done and lead to such great harms that it seems to us impossible that any good result could ever come of them . . . such as the angels who fell out of heaven because of pride . . . and many . . . who live unchristian lives and so die out of God's love.
>
> And all this being so, it seemed to me that it was impossible that every kind of thing should be well, as

our Lord revealed at this time. And to this I had no
other answer as a revelation from our Lord except this:
What is impossible to you is not impossible to me. I
shall preserve my word in everything, and I shall make
everything well.[91]

Loving people in the name of Jesus is slow, hard work. At
times, fruit emerges slowly—very slowly. But the love of God,
who promises us "all will be well," offers us power, sustenance,
and the long-term perspective we need to remain faithful.

Question to Consider

God said to Julian, "All will be well, and all will be well, and
every kind of thing will be well." In what relationship or circumstance in your own life do you most need to receive this
promise from God?

Prayer

*Father, from the beginning of time, you have not stopped
pouring out your love to the world. And you continue to
saturate each of us in your love each day. Help me to deeply
receive your love today, and to trust that you will make all
things well, in this world and in the world to come. Help me
to be an extension of your love to those around me today. In
Jesus' name, amen.*

Conclude with Silence (2 minutes)

DAY 4 MORNING/MIDDAY OFFICE

Silence and Stillness before God (2 minutes)

Scripture Reading: 1 John 4:7–8, 16b, 19–20

Dear friends, let us love one another, for love comes from God. Everyone who loves has been born of God and knows God. Whoever does not love does not know God, because God is love. . . .

Whoever lives in love lives in God, and God in them. . . .

We love because he first loved us. Whoever claims to love God yet hates a brother or sister is a liar. For whoever does not love their brother and sister, whom they have seen, cannot love God, whom they have not seen.

Devotional

In his classic book, *Spiritual Friendship*, twelfth-century Cistercian monk Aelred of Rievaulx wrote that friendship, especially between believers, is a direct path to God, not a diversion from it. Paraphrasing a portion of the passage from 1 John, he wrote, "God is friendship, and he that abides in friendship abides in God." Aelred's seminal insight on God's love has been examined by theologians for centuries. Why? Because when he substituted the word *friendship* for *love,* he highlighted a unique aspect of Jesus' love—specifically, when he calls us *friends* (John 15:14).

As we move toward people to offer the love of Jesus, we too extend to them a true spiritual friendship distinct from that of the world. It is a friendship that reflects Jesus' friendship to us. Here is how Aelred describes what it's like to love as a true spiritual friend:

> But what happiness, what security, what joy to have some-one to whom you dare to speak on terms of equality as to another self; one to whom you need have no fear to confess your failings; one to whom you can unblushingly make known what progress you have made in the spiritual life; one to whom you can entrust all the secrets of your heart and before whom you can place all your plans![92]

In other words, when the love of God is present in friend-ship, we cease to treat people as a means to an end. We lay aside any desire to "get something." We affirm and appreciate their uniqueness. And we acknowledge our mutual brokenness and weakness. In a social media world where so much time is spent managing one's "personal brand" and consistently appearing happy, this type of friendship is a rare gift.

Question to Consider

How might you be a true spiritual friend to someone in your life this week?

Prayer

Jesus, thank you for calling me a friend. It is almost too much to take in! Teach me to be a true friend—to you and to others.

Grant me the desire and the power to listen with my whole heart, renouncing my own agenda, and appreciating the uniqueness of each individual I come in contact with today. In Jesus' name, amen.

Conclude with Silence (2 minutes)

DAY 4 MIDDAY/EVENING OFFICE

Silence and Stillness before God (2 minutes)

Scripture Reading: Psalm 46:1–6, 10a

> God is our refuge and strength,
>> an ever-present help in trouble.
> Therefore we will not fear, though the earth give way
>> and the mountains fall into the heart of the sea,
> though its waters roar and foam
>> and the mountains quake with their surging.
> There is a river whose streams make glad the city
> of God,
>> the holy place where the Most High dwells.
> God is within her, she will not fall;
>> God will help her at break of day.
> Nations are in uproar, kingdoms fall;
>> he lifts his voice, the earth melts. . . .
> He says, "Be still, and know that I am God."

Devotional

Silence and solitude are perhaps the most challenging and least practiced spiritual disciplines among Christians today. We live in a world of noise and distractions. Most of us fear silence. Yet when we look at the life of Jesus, we observe him regularly withdrawing to lonely places to be still and pray (Luke 5:16). We find biblical greats like Moses, Elijah, and John the Baptist spent *decades* alone with God before launching their public ministry. Where did they get such power to love when the world around them was falling apart? How were they able to love people who opposed them and were not responsive, and over so many years! We can be sure it was born and nurtured out of a deep relationship with God that included intentional times of listening and communing in stillness and silence.

Spending time in silence and stillness with God is a necessary and valuable counterweight to the thoughtless and excessive words we are routinely exposed to in the world. Stepping out of the noise of life through a daily practice of silence is actually a radical and prophetic act. It is also one we are in danger of losing. Author Gunilla Norris says it well:

> Silence reveals. Silence heals. Silence is where God dwells. We yearn to be there.... [And yet] in our present culture, silence is an endangered species ... an endangered fundamental. We need it badly. Silence brings us back to basics, to our senses, to our selves. It locates us. Without that return

we can go so far away from our true natures that we end up, quite literally, beside ourselves. . . .

The experience of silence is now so rare that we must cultivate it and treasure it.[93]

God offers us an inexhaustible well of living water in Jesus to love people over the long haul of our lives. However, in order to drink from that well, we must learn to integrate silence and stillness as foundational spiritual disciplines in our lives.

Question to Consider

How might you create additional space in your life for silence today?

Prayer

Lord, help me to be still and wait patiently for you in silence today. I know that you are always present with me and that you delight to spend time with me. Out of my silence and resting in your love, I ask that you enable me to see the people around me as you do—as unrepeatable and precious. In Jesus' name, amen.

Conclude with Silence (2 minutes)

DAY 5 MORNING/MIDDAY PRAYER

Silence and Stillness before God (2 minutes)

Scripture Reading: Psalm 139:13–16

> For you created my inmost being;
>> you knit me together in my mother's womb.
>
> I praise you because I am fearfully and wonderfully made;
>> your works are wonderful,
>> I know that full well.
>
> My frame was not hidden from you
>> when I was made in the secret place,
>> when I was woven together in the depths of the earth.
>
> Your eyes saw my unformed body;
>> all the days ordained for me were written in your book
>> before one of them came to be.

Devotional

God created us in his image, knit us together in our mother's womb with great care, and chose us for a special purpose on earth. Jesus sets us on the path to this purpose with this summary of Scripture: "to love the Lord your God with all your heart and with all your soul and with all your mind . . . and to "love your neighbor as yourself" (Matthew 22:37–40).

As you come to the end of this devotional, prayerfully consider the specific ways God is inviting you to love others well. Consider these wise words from my wife, Geri, on the importance of discerning God's specific plans for each of us.

> One way we discern our distinctive life is from the perspective of discovering our "sealed orders" from God. Sealed

orders, historically, refer to specific written instructions given, for example, to the captain of a ship regarding his destination or mission. They are not to be opened until a specified time or place is reached. It is as if God has given each one of us sealed orders for our lives. . . . Author Sheila Linn simply and profoundly describes this process: "When I am in touch with the special purpose of my life in carrying out my sealed orders, I have a profound feeling of consolation or rightness and my whole body relaxes. I believe the sense of rightness expresses itself physiologically because the purpose of our life is built into the very cells of our body."[94]

These "sealed orders," the special purpose God has for each of us, involve both paying attention to him (even through our body) and paying attention to the Holy Spirit inside us. Our love for others is rooted and grounded in God's hospitality to us in Christ. This reality gives us the courage to take the risk in faith to show kindness to others, whether it be those routinely marginalized by society (the refugee, the poor, the disabled, the stranger) or those close to us who feel unloved, wounded, or rejected. The needs around us are enormous. But we can be thankful God is in charge of the world. We need only to discern our sealed orders.

Question to Consider

Speak to God about your willingness—or unwillingness—to follow his sealed orders, wherever they may lead you. What joys or fears are you aware of?

Prayer

> *Lord, I want to discover your "sealed orders" for me, the unique*
> *purpose you have for me—this day and every day. I am in your*
> *hands, Lord. I love you. Help me to trust you as I offer my life*
> *as a gift to others—today, tomorrow, and for the rest of my life.*
> *In Jesus' name, amen.*

Conclude with Silence (2 minutes)

DAY 5 MIDDAY/EVENING PRAYER

Silence and Stillness before God (2 minutes)

Scripture Reading: Matthew 13:31–32

> He told them another parable: "The kingdom of heaven
> is like a mustard seed, which a man took and planted in
> his field. Though it is the smallest of all seeds, yet when it
> grows, it is the largest of garden plants and becomes a tree,
> so that the birds come and perch in its branches."

Devotional

The way of the world is big and fast. King Herod erected massive
buildings. Rome built a powerful empire. Athens boasted of her
brilliant intellectuals. In contrast, the way of Jesus is slow and
small. Just as the mustard seed begins as something small, the
kingdom of God takes root in the tiny confines of the human
heart but slowly grows into a tree of life—one that connects with
God and others to cover the whole earth.

Jesus wants us to know that if we are to mature as Christ followers, we need to grasp this critical truth. We need to be willing and patient to let him grow us slowly.

Alan Kreider, a church historian, notes that one of the primary reasons the church grew in its first 300 years—through persecutions, oppression, and difficulties—was Christians were committed to patience and perseverance. Whether it was in their business dealings, sexual morality, valuing of women and children, care for the poor, or refusal to participate in violence, they created a comprehensive "culture of patience." In fact, he argues, the early church fathers wrote more about the Christian virtue of patience than about evangelism. He writes:

> God, in dealing with Israel across the centuries, was never in a hurry. . . . The people rejected and killed Jesus, but they did not frustrate God's purposes. God's mission is unhurried and unstoppable. . . . [In fact,] "patience is the very nature of God." . . .
>
> The fall of Adam and Eve was marked by human impatience, which was "the original sin in the eyes of the Lord." . . .
>
> Patience is a distinctive sign of the Christian; it enables believers to live "in the way of Christ" amid the crises of their lives.[95]

People looking on from the outside were attracted to the non-anxious, unforced lifestyle of the early church. Many of us struggle with the slow, mustard-seed nature of the way Jesus works, especially as it relates to personal growth and change. But he promises that if we faithfully remain with him, we too will discover that the mustard seed of what God is doing in us will grow remarkably and powerfully. "The kingdom of the world [will] become the kingdom of our Lord and of his Messiah, and he will reign for ever and ever" (Revelation 11:15). And that transformation will include us as well—if we patiently persevere with him.

Question to Consider

In what one area of your life might God be inviting you to patiently trust him today?

Prayer

> *Enter, O my Light, and enlighten my darkness;*
> *Enter, O my Life, and resurrect my deadness;*
> *Enter, O my Physician, and heal my wounds;*
> *Enter, O Divine Fire, and burn up the thorns of my sins;*
> *Ignite my inward parts and my heart with the flame of Thy love;*
> *Enter, O my King, and destroy in me the kingdom of sin;*
> *Sit on the throne of my heart and reign in me alone,*
> *O Thou, my King and Lord.*

—Dimitri of Rostov, seventeenth-century Russian bishop

Conclude with Silence (2 minutes)

Appendix A: The Lord's Prayer

Meditate on each phrase.
Take your time; pause after each line.

Our
Father in heaven,
Hallowed be your name,
Your kingdom come.
Your will be done
On earth as it is in heaven.
Give us this day our daily bread.
Forgive us our trespasses
As we forgive those who trespass against us;
And lead us not into temptation,
But deliver us from evil ("the evil one").

Appendix B: Breath Prayer

Breath prayer is an ancient Christian practice dating back to at least the early centuries of the church. The famous "Jesus Prayer" is an example of a breath prayer. Developed from the parable of the Pharisee and the Tax Collector in Luke 18:9–14, it is drawn from the tax collector's desperate plea for mercy: "Lord Jesus Christ, Son of God, have mercy on me, a sinner." Each phrase of the prayer is prayed under the breath on an inhale or exhale. I have found breath prayer to be an especially helpful practice when I feel distracted as I come to be silent and still before the Lord.

Breath prayer is similar to silent prayer in that it can be done at any time, for we are always breathing! In Scripture, breath is a metaphor for the Spirit of God. It is through breath that God gives life (Genesis 2:7) and it is through breath that Jesus gives the Holy Spirit (John 20:22).

The following are a few guidelines[96] to help you practice breath prayer:

- Sit upright in a silent place. Draw your attention to your breathing.

- Breathe from your diaphragm, allowing your abdomen to rise and fall easily. Don't force your breath or breathe too quickly.
- Whenever your thoughts wander, bring your attention back to your breath. As you inhale, ask God to fill you with the Spirit of life. As you exhale, release anything that is not of him.
- When your time of silence is over, pause to thank God for your time with him.

Appendix C: Top Ten FAQs about Practicing Silence

1. Why is practicing silence so hard?

Imagine having never exercised your entire life and then trying to sprint a mile. It would be very difficult. However, if you continued to practice, it would get much easier over time. The same is true when it comes to exercising the spiritual muscle that enables you to pay attention to God through silence. It is God who commands us to be still in his presence (Psalm 37:7; 46:10). This means God has also given us the capacity to attend to him in this way. In fact, every human being has a contemplative dimension that actually longs for silence with God. A relationship with God requires that we stop talking all the time so we can develop the capacity to simply enjoy being with him.

2. How is spending time in silence different from Eastern meditation, New Age practices, or secular programs on mindfulness?

We should not be surprised that other religions utilize the practice of silence. Many other faiths also have communal worship, sacred texts or scriptures, and spiritual disciplines, etc. The significant difference between Christian meditation and other kinds of meditation is that we are not attempting to empty our minds into nothingness or to achieve an altered state of consciousness. Instead, we practice silence to focus our minds on God and to spend time in his presence. This type of prayer is not new or New Age. Its roots extend as far back in Scripture as Moses and Elijah, continue into the New Testament with John the Baptist and Jesus, and have persisted throughout more than two thousand years of Christian history. In silence we are simply being with the God of Abraham, Isaac, and Jacob. Moreover, this kind of prayer is part of our larger prayer life that includes worship, confession, petitions, etc.

3. How much time should I spend in silence each day?

I used to recommend beginning with two minutes a day, but lately I've been recommending that people start with five minutes a day and slowly increase the time until they are spending ten to twenty minutes each day in silence. My practice is to spend twenty minutes in silence as part of my morning Office (time of prayer). For me, early morning—before the activities of the day begin—is best, but that is not possible for everyone. I also integrate briefer times (one to ten minutes) of silence during my midday and evening Offices. A great deal of research over the last fifteen years has confirmed how silence and meditation rewires our brains, helping us become more aware, more empathic, and reducing stress.[97]

4. What can I do when my mind wanders?

This is the number one challenge for most people. You are not alone! Our minds can wander a hundred times in a five-minute period. Here are the three things I do when my mind wanders. First, before entering silence, I spend time reading Scripture, a devotional passage, or writing in a journal if I have a lot on my mind. This helps to focus and settle my thoughts before I begin my time of silence. Second, when my thoughts wander, I redirect my attention to my breathing, focusing on both inhalation and exhalation as gifts of God. Focusing on the rhythm of breathing in and out is a practice used quite a bit among Orthodox Christians and is commonly talked about in secular settings as a tool for developing "mindfulness." And finally, I focus on one word, such as Abba or Jesus, to refocus my conscious thoughts on Christ. This helps to keep me anchored in him.

5. What should I do if I don't have a quiet place at home or at work?

It is possible to experience interior silence even when we are unable to have exterior silence. Believe it or not, I have practiced silence in such noisy places as Times Square, subway trains, city buses, airplanes, stairwells, park benches, highway rest stops, my car, on the beach, and empty church buildings. I know school-teachers who use closets, sanitation workers who use their trucks, and students who use libraries.

6. *What would help me to grow in this practice?*

I sometimes light a candle as a symbol of Christ's presence with me. I use the timer on my phone each morning, setting it for twenty minutes. At other times of the day, I may set it for three or five minutes depending on my time constraints. Scripture is a core component of my time with God—either before or after my time of silence. Meditating on, memorizing, studying, and reading Scripture have become so much richer for me as I have created ample space to be still. I also have a special chair I use in my office, giving me a sense of sacred space that is set apart.

7. *Am I doing it wrong if I don't I hear God speak when I am silent?*

The goal of spending time in silence is not necessarily to hear from God but to be with God. When I spend time in silence, I am not looking for guidance, though it often comes. However, I do find that God says a lot when I am quiet! Part of maturing in Christ is not judging the quality of our time with him based on how we feel. The goal is to be with Jesus, not to have a "feel-good" experience. And the benefits of spending time in silence go beyond the time itself (for example, greater awareness of God and ourselves throughout the day, feeling more centered and less triggered, having a deeper sense of peacefulness, etc.). Just showing up to consistently be with Jesus in silence is an expression of trust and dependence on him.

8. *What do I do if I don't have enough time and feel rushed?*

I adjust to the time I have allotted. For example, if I have only ten minutes for midday prayer, I structure the limited time I have based on what I need in order to commune with Jesus. This may include more or less silence, reading of Scripture, etc. The goal is not to "get through" a reading or the time set aside for silence. Our aim is to be with Jesus with whatever time we have.

9. *What should I do if I've practiced silence for a while but feel bored and want to quit?*

There is a great deal to learn about the interior movements of your heart and silence with God. Getting started is often the most difficult step, much like starting an exercise routine or any other new habit that requires some planning and effort. However, if you stick with it, chances are you will wonder—as have so many others before you—how you ever lived without it. If you're feeling bored, I encourage you to seek out additional inspiration and resources. You might begin by looking at the Centering Prayer materials of Thomas Keating (available online at www.contemplative outreach.org). And I would encourage you to look up the many evangelical authors who are now writing on the integration of silence, stillness, and solitude in the midst of our very active lives.

10. *Why should I practice silence every day? Isn't once or twice a year on retreat enough?*

Retreats are wonderful opportunities for us to "get away" from our routines and a powerful means to progress in our relationship with Jesus. An important question to ask on every retreat is what adjustments God might have for our lives. For example, How might I need to adjust my rhythms with God? What is his invitation for me in this next season? The fruit of retreats is to be found in our everyday practices.

I believe a daily practice of silence and stillness is needed for all of us. Why? Our goal is to cultivate our personal relationship with him—to be with God—surrendering our will to his will, our presence to his presence, and our actions to his actions each day. For this reason, silence and stillness with God are a foundational practice by which we actually position ourselves for God to do his transformative work in us.

Appendix D: Compline: Praying Before You Go to Sleep

Compline (pronounced "comp-line" or "comp-lin"), a going-to-sleep prayer of trust, is a wonderful way to end the day with God. For people like you and me who live outside a monastic community, it is the last of four daily Offices typically observed during the following time frames:

Morning Prayer: 6:00 a.m. – 9:00 a.m.
Afternoon Prayer: 11:00 a.m. – 2:00 p.m.
Evening Prayer: 5:00 p.m. – 8:00 p.m.
Compline: just before going to sleep

While I occasionally miss one or more of these in a day (especially Evening Prayer), the structure and flexibility of these time frames have transformed my spiritual life since I began observing the Offices in 2003. My Morning Prayer, for example, tends to be much longer than Afternoon or Evening Prayer, but the reminder to pause, even for only a few minutes, helps me remember God as the source, center, and goal of my life.

Compline is observed right before you go to sleep and is

meant to be brief. You may read a portion of a Psalm (such as Psalm 31, 91, 131, or 134), do the Examen (review of the day with God), or pray the Lord's Prayer. I often use this simple prayer from *The Book of Common Prayer*: "May the Lord grant me and those I love a peaceful night and a perfect end." When Geri and I pray this together, we insert the names of each of our daughters, son-in-law, and grandchild after the phrase "those we love."

The particular beauty I appreciate most about Compline is the way it brackets my day with God. I begin with Morning Prayer and end with Compline. When I close my eyes to sleep, I release to God all the unfinished work of the day and trust him with my life. I am reminded of the fragileness of life and my dependence on him. When my eyes close to sleep, I am profoundly aware I may awake to see him face-to-face because he has called me home. Otherwise, I will awake the following morning to serve him for another day on earth.

Notes

1. Peter and Geri Scazzero, *The Emotionally Healthy Relationships Workbook* and *The Emotionally Healthy Relationships DVD* (Grand Rapids: Zondervan, 2017).
2. For more information about the Daily Office, see ch. 6 in Peter Scazzero, *Emotionally Healthy Spirituality: It's Impossible to Be Spiritually Mature While Remaining Emotionally Immature* (Grand Rapids: Zondervan, 2017), 139–48.
3. Timothy Fry, ed., *RB 1980: The Rule of St. Benedict in English* (Collegeville, Minn.: Liturgical Press, 1981), 65.
4. The course includes the *Emotionally Healthy Relationships Workbook* and the accompanying *Emotionally Healthy Relationships DVD*.
5. For a fuller explanation of loving union, see ch. 4, "Slow Down for Loving Union," in Peter Scazzero, *The Emotionally Healthy Leader: How Transforming Your Inner Life Will Deeply Transform Your Church, Team, and the World* (Grand Rapids: Zondervan, 2015), 115–42.
6. For additional resources such as videos, a downloadable wallet card, and testimonies of those who have

benefited from practicing the Daily Office, visit www .emotionallyhealthy.org.

7. Brother Lawrence, *The Practice of the Presence of God* (Old Tappan, N.J.: Revell, 1958), 29, 36.

8. Jean Vanier, *From Brokenness to Community* (Mahwah, N.J.: Paulist Press, 1992), 15–19.

9. Henri J. M. Nouwen, *Return of the Prodigal Son: A Meditation on Fathers, Brothers, and Sons* (New York: Doubleday, 1992), 66–67.

10. Geffrey B. Kelly and F. Burton Nelson, eds., *A Testament to Freedom: The Essential Writings of Dietrich Bonhoeffer* (New York: HarperCollins, 1990, 1995), 332–33.

11. Cited in James Bryan Smith, *Embracing the Love of God: The Path and Promise of Christian Life* (New York: HarperCollins, 2010), 13.

12. Quoted in Rowan Williams, *Where God Happens: Discovering Christ in One Another* (Boston: Shambhala, 2005), 13–14.

13. *The Sayings of the Desert Fathers: The Alphabetical Collection*, trans. Benedicta Ward (Kalamazoo, Mich.: Cistercian Publications, 1975), 75.

14. Maximus the Confessor, quoted in George Berhold, *Maximus the Confessor: Selected Writings, Classics of Western Spirituality* (Mahwah, N.J.: Paulist Press, 1985), 86.

15. *Finding God in All Things: A Marquette Prayer Book* (Milwaukee: Marquette University Press, 2009), 50, 100.

16. John O'Donohue, *To Bless the Space Between Us: A Book of Blessings* (New York: Doubleday, 2008), 49.

17. St. Teresa of Avila, *Life of Prayer*, ed. James M. Houston (Colorado Springs: David C. Cook, 2006), 253.

18. For additional information, see Colleen Carroll Campbell, *My Sisters the Saints: A Spiritual Memoir* (New York: Image, 2012), 35–36.

19. St. Thérèse of Lisieux, *The Story of a Soul: A New Translation*, trans. and ed. Robert J. Edmonson, CJ (Brewster, Mass.: Paraclete Press, 2006), 230, 164.

20. Stephen Payne OCD, and Phyllis Zagano, *The Carmelite Tradition,* Spirituality in History Series (Collegeville, Minn.: Order of St. Benedict, 2011), 124.

21. This simple list is my summary of key points from two excellent books on the nuances and benefits of silence by Maggie Ross: *Silence: A User's Guide, Vol. 1: Process* (Eugene, Ore.: Wipf and Stock, 2014); and *Writing the Icon of the Heart: In Silence Beholding* (Eugene, Ore.: Wipf and Stock, 2013).

22. For a fuller exploration of how such lying destroys our relationship with God, ourselves, and others, see Geri Scazzero, *The Emotionally Healthy Woman: Eight Things You Have to Quit to Change Your Life* (Grand Rapids: Zondervan, 2010), 45–62.

23. For a fuller exploration of this theme of faulty thinking, see Geri Scazzero, *The Emotionally Healthy Woman*, 167–90.

24. Thomas Merton, *New Seeds of Contemplation* (New York: New Directions, 1987), 14.

25. For more information, see Scazzero, *Emotionally Healthy Spirituality*, 178–85.

26. Eugene H. Peterson, *Leap Over a Wall: Earthly Spirituality for Everyday Christians* (San Francisco: HarperCollins, 1997), 162–63.

27. For additional guidance, see Geri Scazzero, *The Emotionally Healthy Woman*, ch. 5, "Quit Blaming," 115–40.

28. See Joshua Wolf Shenk, *Lincoln's Melancholy: How Depression Challenged a President and Fueled His Greatness* (New York: Houghton Mifflin, 2005).

29. For a fuller exploration of this truth, see *Emotionally Healthy Spirituality*, 137–52.

30. Peter Scazzero, *The Emotionally Healthy Leader*, 204–205.

31. Kaethe Weingarten, "Witnessing the Effects of Political Violence in Families: Mechanisms of Intergenerational Transmission and Clinical Interventions," *Journal of Marital and Family Therapy*, January 2004, vol. 30, no. 1, 49–51.

32. Quoted in Bonnie Thurston, *Hidden in God: Discovering the Desert Vision of Charles De Foucauld* (Notre Dame, Ind.: Ave Maria Press, 2016), xiii.

33. Alicia Britt Chole, *Anonymous: Jesus' Hidden Years and Yours* (Nashville: Thomas Nelson, 2006), 8–10, 12–13, 27.

34. Walter Brueggemann, *Genesis: Interpretation Bible Commentary for Preaching and Teaching* (Atlanta: John Knox Press, 1982), 293, 376.

35. Phillips Brooks, *The Candle of the Lord and Other Sermons, Second Series* (New York: E. P. Dutton and Company, 1910), 10.

36. Viktor E. Frankl, *Man's Search for Meaning: An Introduction to Logotherapy* (New York: Simon and Schuster, 1959) 82, 84–85, 88, 109.

37. Eugene H. Peterson, *The Jesus Way: A Conversation on the Ways of Jesus* (Grand Rapids: Eerdmanns, 2007), 97.

38. St. Teresa of Avila, *Life of Prayer*, 253.

39. For more information, see Peter Scazzero, *The Emotionally Healthy Church: A Strategy for Discipleship That Actually Changes Lives, Updated and Expanded Edition* (Grand Rapids: Zondervan, 2010), 33, 55–56.

40. Philip Yancey, *Disappointment with God: Three Questions No One Asks Aloud* (Grand Rapids: Zondervan, 1992), 263.

41. See Geri Scazzero, *The Emotionally Healthy Woman*, 91–93.

42. Thomas H. Green, *Weeds Among the Wheat: Discernment: Where Prayer and Action Meet* (Notre Dame, Ind.: Ave Maria Press, 1984), 22.

43. Dan B. Allender and Tremper Longman III, *The Cry of the Soul: How Our Emotions Reveal Our Deepest Questions about God* (Dallas: Word, 1994), 21–23.

44. Peter Storey, *With God in the Crucible: Preaching Costly Discipleship* (Nashville: Abington Press, 2002), 12.

45. Dietrich Bonhoeffer, *Life Together: The Classic Exploration of Christian Community* (New York: Harper and Row, 1954), 29.

46. Quoted in Arthur Boers, *Living into Focus: Choosing What Matters in an Age of Distractions* (Grand Rapids: Brazos Press, 2012), 185.

47. Alice Fryling, *Seeking God Together: An Introduction to Group Spiritual Direction* (Downers Grove, Ill.: InterVarsity Press, 2009), 63–64.

48. For a larger treatment of a practical theology for anger, see Geri Scazzero, *The Emotionally Healthy Woman*, 94–100.

49. Aristotle. Cited at www.wisdomquotes.com/quote/aristotle-10.html.

50. Richard Rohr, *Hope Against Darkness: The Transforming Vision of St. Francis in an Age of Anxiety* (Cincinnati: Franciscan Media, 2001), 38–39.

51. http://www.motherteresa.org/07_family/family00.html.

52. David Scott, *The Love That Made Mother Teresa: How Her Secret Visions and Dark Nights Can Help You Conquer the Slums of Your Heart*, Special Canonization Edition (Manchester, N.H.: Sophia Press, 2016), 48.

53. Mother Teresa, *Words to Love By* (Notre Dame, Ind.: Ave Maria Press, 1983), 80.

54. Josef Pieper, *Faith, Hope, Love* (San Francisco: St. Ignatius Press, 1997), 174, 176.

55. William E. Kaufman, *Contemporary Jewish Philosophies* (Detroit: Wayne State University Press, 1976), 62–63.

56. Martin Buber, *Between Man and Man* (New York: Routledge, 2002), 16.

57. For additional insights on the impact this event had
    on Buber, see Kenneth Paul Kramer with Mechthild
    Gawlick, *Martin Buber's I and Thou: Practicing Living
    Dialogue* (Mahwah, N.J.: Paulist Press, 2003), 174–75.

58. Henri J. M. Nouwen, *Out of Solitude: Three Meditations
    on the Christian Life* (Notre Dame, Ind.: Ave Maria Press,
    1974), 31–32, 36.

59. Scazzero, *Emotionally Healthy Spirituality*, 183.

60. Jonathan Edwards, *Heaven: A World of Love* (North
    Charleston, S.C.: CreateSpace Independent Publishing
    Platform, 2013), 4.

61. Eugene H. Peterson, "Introduction to Job," *The Message:
    The Bible in Contemporary Language* (Colorado Springs:
    NavPress, 2002), 633–34.

62. Parker J. Palmer, *A Hidden Wholeness: The Journey
    Toward an Undivided Life* (San Francisco: Jossey Bass,
    2004), 146. Over 300 years ago, the Quakers developed
    an intentional discernment practice they called a
    "clearness committee." I have learned a great deal about
    this listening practice over the years from Parker Palmer's
    organization, the Center for Courage and Renewal. For
    additional information about the center and clearness
    committees, visit www.couragerenewal.org.

63. Henri J. M. Nouwen, *The Wounded Healer: In Our Own
    Woundedness, We Can Become a Source of Life for Others*
    (New York: Image Books, 1979), 72.

64. Leighton Ford, *The Attentive Life: Discerning God's*

Presence in All Things (Downers Grove, Ill.: InterVarsity Press, 2008), 23–24.

65. For additional teaching on saying no, see *The Emotionally Healthy Woman*, 127–28.

66. See Frederick Dale Brunner, *The Gospel of John: A Commentary* (Grand Rapids: Eerdmans, 2012), 62–70, 86.

67. Frederick Buechner, *Listening to Your Life: Daily Meditations with Frederick Buechner* (San Francisco: HarperSanFrancisco, 1992), 184–85.

68. Parker Palmer, *Let Your Life Speak: Listening for the Voice of Vocation* (San Francisco: Jossey Bass, 2000), 32–33.

69. For additional material on this theme, see ch. 8, "Quit Living Someone Else's Life," in Scazzero, *The Emotionally Healthy Woman*, 210.

70. Chuck Yeager and Leo Janos, *Yeager: An Autobiography* (New York: Bantam Books, 1985), 154.

71. *Yeager: An Autobiography*, 165.

72. Henri J. M. Nouwen, *Can You Drink the Cup?* (Notre Dame, Ind.: Ave Maria, 1996), 28.

73. M. Robert Mulholland Jr., *The Deeper Journey: The Spirituality of Discovering Your True Self* (Downers Grove, Ill.: InterVarsity Press, 2006), 31, 37, 39, 45.

74. For additional teaching on this important theme, see ch. 6, "Quit Overfunctioning," in Scazzero, *The Emotionally Healthy Woman*.

75. For an extended discussion on differentiation, see Scazzero, *Emotionally Healthy Spirituality*, 82, 90.

76. Palmer, *A Hidden Wholeness*, 15–16, 20.

77. For a fuller treatment of true peacemaking, see Scazzero, *Emotionally Healthy Spirituality*, 184–86.

78. Walter Brueggemann, *The Message of the Psalms: A Theological Commentary* (Minneapolis: Augsburg, 1984), 9–11, 19.

79. David G. Benner, *Soulful Spirituality: Becoming Fully Alive and Deeply Human* (Grand Rapids: Brazos Press, 2011), 166–67.

80. John Paul Lederach, *Reconcile: Conflict Transformation for Ordinary Christians* (Harrisonburg, Pa.: Herald Press, 2014), 37, 42, 55.

81. Margaret Guenther, *At Home in the World: A Rule of Life for the Rest of Us* (New York: Seabury Books, 2006), 68–69.

82. Robert Coles, *Dorothy Day: A Radical Devotion* (Boston: Da Capo Press, 1987), xviii.

83. *The Desert Fathers: Sayings of the Early Christian Monks*, trans. Benedicta Ward (New York: Penguin Classics, 2003), 172.

84. This story is cited and further amplified in Scazzero, *The Emotionally Healthy Leader*, 64.

85. His story is recounted throughout Henri J. M. Nouwen, *In the Name of Jesus: Reflections on Christian Leadership* (New York: Crossroad Publishing Company, 1991).

86. The original version of Meninger's prayer can also be found in his book, William A. Meninger, *The Process of Forgiveness* (New York: Continuum Press, 1996), 123.

87. Quoted in Laurel A. Dykstra, "A Harsh and Dreadful Love,"
    Sojourners (www.sojo.net), September/October 2008.
88. Quoted in Gordon J. Wenham, *Numbers: An
    Introduction and Commentary* (Downers Grove, Ill.:
    InterVarsity Press, 1981), 151.
89. Henri J. M. Nouwen, *Life of the Beloved: Spiritual Living
    in a Secular World* (New York: Crossroad, 1992), 49, 53,
    67, 75, 86–87, 105, 112.
90. C. S. Lewis, *The Voyage of the Dawn Treader*, The
    Chronicles of Narnia (New York: Collier, 1970), 90–91.
91. *Julian of Norwich Showings: The Classics of Western
    Spirituality*, trans. and introduction, Edmund Colledge
    and James Walsh, S.J. (Mahwah, N.J.: Paulist Press,
    1978), 225–26, 232–33.
92. Aelred of Rievaulx, *Spiritual Friendship*, trans. Mary
    Eugenia Laker (Kalamazoo, Mich.: Cistercian, 1974), 66.
93. Gunilla Norris, *Inviting Silence: Universal Principles of
    Meditation* (New York: Blue Bridge Books, 2004), 8, 31, 79.
94. Geri Scazzero, *The Emotionally Healthy Woman*, 196.
95. Alan Kreider, *The Patient Ferment of the Early Church:
    The Improbable Rise of Christianity in the Roman Empire*
    (Grand Rapids: Baker, 2016), 18–19, 22, 30.
96. These guidelines are adapted from Daniel Wolpert,
    *Leading a Life with God: The Practice of Spiritual
    Leadership*, 2006. For additional resources on breath
    prayer, see Richard Foster's *Prayer: Finding the Heart's
    True Home* (New York: HarperCollins, 1992) and

Marykate Morse's *A Guidebook to Prayer: 24 Ways to Walk with God* (Downers Grove, Ill.: InterVarsity, 2013). For an Orthodox perspective, see "Jesus Prayer: Breathing Exercises," by Bishop Kallistos-Ware, orthodoxprayer.org.

97. See, for example, Andrew Newberg and Mark Robert Waldman, *How God Changes Your Brain* (New York: Ballantine, 2009); and Mayo Clinic, "Meditation: A Simple, Fast Way to Reduce Stress," www.mayoclinic.com.

We Help Church Leaders Make Mature Disciples

Move your people from shallow Christianity to depth in Christ.

Developed over the last 21 years, *The Emotionally Healthy Discipleship Course* is a strategy for discipleship that is proven to change lives not just on the surface, but deeply. People in your church begin working out conflicts and grow in unity. You're able to identify and develop your future leaders. And ultimately, your church makes a greater impact in the world for Christ.

EMOTIONALLY HEALTHY SPIRITUALITY

Introducing people to a transformative spirituality with God.

EMOTIONALLY HEALTHY RELATIONSHIPS

Practical skills to launch people into a transformative spirituality with others.

ZONDERVAN®

It's Time to Get Started!
Here Are Your 3 Steps:

GET THE KIT
Includes everything you need to run the course

9780310101352

GET TRAINED
Attend Online Training and discover how to lead the course
emotionallyhealthy.org/lead

RUN THE COURSE
Run a pilot group through both parts of the course

 emotionally HEALTHY DISCIPLESHIP   **ZONDERVAN**

Leader's Resource Vault

Access a treasure chest of exclusive content designed to equip you to lead *The Emotionally Healthy Discipleship Course* effectively in your church or ministry.

In the Leader's Resource Vault you and your team will receive:

- Planning timelines
- Session schedules
- Training videos and resources
- Presentation decks
- Certificates of completion for participants
- Top 25 FAQ's people ask
- Marketing & promotional graphics

Access to a Certified EH Discipleship Course Coach:

- Customize a plan for your specific ministry context
- Build on areas of strength in your ministry
- Receive specific tools to ensure the Course develops disciple-makers and leaders

Exclusive Resources:
- Have your ministry posted publicly on a national map
- Access to Online Q&A session with author Pete Scazzero
- Networking with other Point Leaders in an EHD Private Facebook Group

Get access today at:
EmotionallyHealthy.org/Vault

Bestselling author Peter Scazzero shows leaders how to develop a deep, inner life with Christ, examining its profound implications for surviving stress, planning and decision making, building teams, creating healthy culture, influencing others, and much more.

Going beyond simply offering a quick fix or new technique, *The Emotionally Healthy Leader* gets to the core, beneath-the-surface issues of uniquely Christian leadership. This book is more than a book you will read; it is a resource you will come back to over and over again.

THE EMOTIONALLY HEALTHY LEADER

How Transforming Your Inner Life Will Deeply Transform Your Church, Team, and the World

9780310494577

Available now at your favorite bookstore.

In this updated and expanded edition of his Gold Medallion Award-winning book, Scazzero shares refreshing new insights and a different and challenging slant on what it takes to lead your congregation to wholeness and maturity in Christ.

Our churches are in trouble, says Scazzero. They are filled with people who are:

- Unsure how to biblically integrate anger, sadness, and other emotions
- Defensive, incapable of revealing their weaknesses
- Threatened by or intolerant of different viewpoints
- Zealous about ministering at church but blind to their spouses' loneliness at home
- So involved in "serving" that they fail to take care of themselves
- Prone to withdraw from conflict rather than resolve it

THE EMOTIONALLY HEALTHY CHURCH
A Strategy for Discipleship That Actually Changes Lives

9780310520757

Available now at your favorite bookstore.

To Change Your Life, You Have to Quit!

The journey to emotional health begins by quitting. Geri quit being afraid of what others think. She quit lying. She quit denying her anger and sadness. She quit living someone else's life. When you quit those things that are damaging to your soul or the souls of others, you are freed up to choose other ways of being and relating that are rooted in love and lead to life.

THE EMOTIONALLY HEALTHY WOMAN

Eight Things You Have to Quit to Change Your Life

Softcover: 9780310342304
Workbook: 9780310828228
DVD: 9780310828235

Available now at your favorite bookstore.

Listen on
Apple Podcasts

The Emotionally Healthy Leader Podcast

Join Pete Scazzero (founder of Emotionally Healthy Discipleship) as he discusses Emotionally Healthy Discipleship in the life of every leader.

What listeners are saying:

"This podcast teaches me to be an agent of change in a culture that is defined by "doing" rather than "being." In a culture obsessed with external success…it's refreshing to hear leaders learn to lead out of their overflow of God's love for them that can only be achieved by slowing down to abide in the love of Jesus."
—Reviewer MarineMike NY

"This stuff can save your life, ministry and relationships."
—Reviewer Brent Squires

"These podcasts are worth listening to each and every time they come out. They cut to the core of issues and give you practical steps to be a better leader and a better Christian."
—Reviewer jhamination

"This podcast is the best resource out there I know for helping me fulfill God's plan for myself and his church!"
—Reviewer Pershing

EmotionallyHealthy.org/Podcast

emotionally
HEALTHY DISCIPLESHIP

ZONDERVAN®

Enjoy even more Day by Day!

Emotionally Healthy Spirituality Day by Day—just like its sister devotional, *Emotionally Healthy Relationships Day by Day*—is your guide to more intentional, meaningful, life-changing communion with God.

In the midst of the hustle, we have to create interludes to re-center our hearts on the presence of God. For eight weeks, each morning and evening devotional will help you create that much-needed space for silence and reflection. You will be encouraged with thoughtful readings and questions to consider.

And after each closing prayer, you'll return to your day with a renewed sense of purpose and peace.

Emotionally Healthy Spirituality Day by Day is also available in Spanish, *Espiritualidad emocionalmente sana Día a día*.

EMOTIONALLY HEALTHY SPIRITUALITY DAY BY DAY

A 40-Day Journey with the Daily Office

9780310351665   English
9780829763676   Spanish

Available now at your favorite bookstore.

✓ CHECKLIST | EMOTIONALLY HEALTHY **SPIRITUALITY** COURSE

SESSION #	📖 EHS BOOK	📅30 DAY-BY-DAY	📝 WORKBOOK	⊙ DVD (or live)
1. The Problem of Emotionally Unhealthy Spirituality	☐ Read Chapter 1	☐ Prayerfully read Intro & Week 1	☐ Read Intro and fill out Session 1	☐ Watch Session 1
2. Know Yourself That You May Know God	☐ Read Chapter 2	☐ Prayerfully read Week 2	☐ Fill out Session 2	☐ Watch Session 2
3. Going Back in Order to Go Forward	☐ Read Chapter 3	☐ Prayerfully read Week 3	☐ Fill out Session 3	☐ Watch Session 3
4. Journey through the Wall	☐ Read Chapter 4	☐ Prayerfully read Week 4	☐ Fill out Session 4	☐ Watch Session 4
5. Enlarge Your Soul through Grief and Loss	☐ Read Chapter 5	☐ Prayerfully read Week 5	☐ Fill out Session 5	☐ Watch Session 5
6. Discover the Rhythms of the Daily Office and Sabbath	☐ Read Chapter 6	☐ Prayerfully read Week 6	☐ Fill out Session 6	☐ Watch Session 6
7. Grow into an Emotionally Healthy Adult	☐ Read Chapter 7	☐ Prayerfully read Week 7	☐ Fill out Session 7	☐ Watch Session 7
8. Go the Next Step to Develop a "Rule of Life"	☐ Read Chapter 8	☐ Prayerfully read Week 8	☐ Fill out Session 8	☐ Watch Session 8

Congratulations on completing **The Emotionally Healthy (EH) Spirituality Course**, the first half of The EH Discipleship Courses.

Go to *emotionallyhealthy.org* to receive your **Certificate of Completion.**

emotionally
HEALTHY DISCIPLESHIP

▇ZONDERVAN·